CONTENTS

WITNESSES AND STATEMENTS FOR THE RECORD

Wednesday, June 22, 1994

S. Hrg. 103-796

TARGETED PENSION FUND INVESTMENT FOR ECONOMIC GROWTH AND DEVELOPMENT

HEARING

BEFORE THE

JOINT ECONOMIC COMMITTEE CONGRESS OF THE UNITED STATES

ONE HUNDRED THIRD CONGRESS

SECOND SESSION

June 22, 1994

Printed for the use of the Joint Economic Committee

84-047 U.S. GOVERNMENT PRINTING OFFICE
WASHINGTON: 1994

For sale by the U.S. Government Printing Office
Superintendent of Documents, Congressional Sales Office, Washington, DC 20402
ISBN 0-16-046081-6

JOINT ECONOMIC COMMITTEE

[Created pursuant to Sec. 5(a) of Public Law 304, 79th Congress]

HOUSE OF REPRESENTATIVES

DAVID R. OBEY, Wisconsin,
Chairman
LEE H. HAMILTON, Indiana
FORTNEY PETE STARK, California
KWEISI MFUME, Maryland
RON WYDEN, Oregon
MICHAEL A. ANDREWS, Texas
RICHARD K. ARMEY, Texas
JIM SAXTON, New Jersey
CHRISTOPHER COX, California
JIM RAMSTAD, Minnesota

SENATE

PAUL S. SARBANES, Maryland,
Vice Chairman
EDWARD M. KENNEDY, Massachusetts
JEFF BINGAMAN, New Mexico
CHARLES S. ROBB, Virginia
BYRON L. DORGAN, North Dakota
BARBARA BOXER, California
WILLIAM V. ROTH, JR., Delaware
CONNIE MACK, Florida
LARRY E. CRAIG, Idaho
ROBERT F. BENNETT, Utah

RICHARD McGAHEY, *Executive Director*
LAWRENCE A. HUNTER, *Minority Staff Director*

TARGETED PENSION FUND INVESTMENT FOR ECONOMIC GROWTH AND DEVELOPMENT

WEDNESDAY, JUNE 22, 1994

CONGRESS OF THE UNITED STATES,
JOINT ECONOMIC COMMITTEE,
Washington, DC.

The Committee met, pursuant to notice, at 10:40 a.m., in room SD–628, Dirksen Senate Office Building, the Honorable Barbara Boxer (Member of the Committee) presiding.

Present: Senator Boxer and Representative Saxton.

Also present: Richard McGahey, Executive Director; Michael Calabrese, General Counsel; Caleb Marshall, Press Secretary, Morgan Reynolds, professional staff member.

OPENING STATEMENT OF SENATOR BOXER, MEMBER

SENATOR BOXER. Good morning. This is going to be a very interesting hearing held by the Joint Economic Committee.

I want to take note that I was in the House for ten years and during that time, I had the pleasure of working with Jim Saxton of New Jersey, and I'm very, very pleased that he's here.

I also want to note that we have some students here from Close-Up, New Americans, and I wanted to welcome you.

Raise your hand if you're from Close-Up.

Wonderful. We love having you here.

I want to welcome all of the witnesses and thank them for taking the time to come before this Committee to testify about the important issue of pension fund investments in affordable housing, job creation in small business infrastructure and other economic development projects.

It is not an easy time for those of us who came to Washington to create jobs and rebuild our communities. The deficit era is behind us. But its legacy continues to tie our hands.

The interest on the debt swallows up billions of dollars that could go to incentives for job creation and business growth, to support new technologies, and to build a world-class infrastructure.

Cutting the deficit, which we must still do, means cutting spending, which means capital-starved cities and towns across the nation will see another year go by without the funds to stimulate new business and new housing or to rebuild our crumbling bridges and roads.

President Clinton, in my opinion, is moving us in the right direction.

In the past two years, the President has made some critical investments in education, mass transit, job training and R&D, while working to reduce our deficit. In fact, projections for 1995 show a drop in the deficit of more than 40 percent from earlier projections.

But investments on the scale that will drive real economic growth and build an economy that will be competitive in the 21st century are increasingly difficult.

To address these investment needs, it's clear that we need lots of creative thinking. Today, we will talk about one possible source of funds to make these necessary investments. That is, economically targeted investments, or ETIs, by our Nation's private and public pension funds.

First, let me say that we are not talking about doing good without making money. We are not talking about social investing at below-market rates of return.

What we are talking about is doing well by doing good. We are talking about investing in needy sectors of our communities while providing a real return for investors.

These are win-win investments, the kind I liked to suggest to my clients when I was a stockbroker—a very, very long time ago.

These are investments that will help our economy grow, investments that create jobs while providing solid rates of return.

We're talking about tapping the vast pension resources, which currently exceed $4 trillion, to invest in sound and profitable economic development projects.

And most important, I want to say that I have not forgotten that these pension funds are the hard-earned retirement savings of millions of working Americans. There is no question that these funds cannot be diverted toward economic development at the expense of more profitable investment opportunities.

But I do believe we can have it both ways. Our witnesses today are going to tell us about investments that provide a competitive rate of return while helping to build the health and productivity of our communities.

I want to give you a couple of examples.

The Boilermaker National Pension Trust has invested roughly $200 million, or about 10 percent of its total assets, in something called the Cogeneration Fund. This fund is designed to target investments in electric cogeneration projects; that is, projects using alternative energy sources, such as solar, geothermal, and waste, to generate electric power.

The Cogeneration Fund has a 5-year projected lifetime return of over 14 percent. In fact, the union considers the fund one of its best investments. This partnership is helping to create jobs for the union's workers. It's creating alternative sources of energy that are environmentally sound, and it is profitable for the pension fund.

There are other examples.

In March of this year, two of California's largest pension funds, CalPERS—the California Public Employees Retirement System—and CalSTERS—the California Teachers Retirement System—joined a nonprofit builder and three of California's biggest financial institutions to launch an affordable housing initiative. This project is expected to provide $340 million of construction loans to finance as many as 5000 housing units in California over the next three years.

This is what I call win-win-win investment. The rate of return for the investors is competitive, new affordable housing units will be available to Californians, and the project will stimulate jobs in California's construction industry, and each and every one of you understands California needs jobs.

These kinds of exciting partnerships are what we need to stimulate economic growth and job creation to build our communities.

ETIs by our Nation's pension funds are growing in number. Laws or programs in 22 states encourage ETIs by pension funds.

But ETIs are done almost exclusively by public and union pension funds, and they represent only a fraction of total tax-exempt institutional assets.

ETIs total about $25 to $30 billion out of more than $4 trillion. That is, less than 1 percent.

In contrast, more than $150 billion in pension investments—and this is important—more than $150 billion in pension investments are in foreign assets outside the United States.

Finally, I want to remind everyone what's at stake in these belt-tightening times. We cannot forget what these kinds of investments would mean in real terms to real people in California and across the nation.

ETIs could mean jobs in affordable housing and better, stronger communities.

So it has not been an easy time for those of us wanting to create jobs. But I don't intend to fold up my cards and drop out of the game. I intend, with my good colleagues, to stay in, to fight and strategize, to win.

So I couldn't be more pleased—and I'm going to put the rest of my statement in the record—I couldn't be more pleased than to see Secretary Reich here. We're going to see Secretary Cisneros. I think we're going to have an excellent hearing.

I really do believe that we're going to see some changes after this hearing, because a lot of people haven't really thought about these things. And once they think about them and they investigate them, we're going to have a whole new avenue of growth in this country.

At this time, I'd ask my colleague for his opening statement, Congressman Saxton from New Jersey.

[The written opening statement of Senator Boxer starts on p. 45 of Submissions for the Record:]

OPENING STATEMENT OF REPRESENTATIVE SAXTON, MEMBER

REPRESENTATIVE SAXTON. Thank you, Senator Boxer. It's good to be here with you again.

I would also like to welcome Secretary Reich and Assistant Secretary Berg. I'm very pleased that you've been willing to come here to discuss this issue with us today, because it certainly is an issue that deserves, in fact demands, full and open discussion.

We're here today to discuss a far-reaching proposal which could have far-reaching effects on our pension system as we know it today.

While we're all social-minded and want our collective lot in life to improve, it is clear that the primary function of a retirement income security system is, and should be, to provide benefits to participants and to their beneficiaries.

This Administration's policy, as outlined by Secretary Reich's written testimony, which I have read in its entirety, establishes an additional objective for America's private pension systems.

In his testimony, Secretary Reich says:

> Pension funds, their dollars reaching 900 times to and from the moon, are positioned like no other force in the American economy to raise income and spark new jobs.

Yes, while the current system of investment of pension funds helps our economy grow when invested with due diligence and in prudent ways to establish a new and additional stated goal, it would give fiduciaries a new, stated objective. And this, in and of itself, would change the role of the investor.

I'd like to quote parenthetically from an article which I recently read entitled, "Economically Targeted Investments–A New Threat to Private Pension Funds," by Wayne Marr of Clemson University, John Nofzinger, and John Tribble of Washington State University. They say in their article:

> In addition to financing the nation's infrastructure, ETI programs could include financing for affordable housing, local and regional job-creating projects, emerging technologies such as fiber optics and telecommunications systems, environmental industries, small businesses, community development banks, and even child care facilities.

It seems to me that we should remind ourselves, and at least in this discussion, talk about these issues, when it comes to the primary objective of those who are charged with the fiduciary responsibility of administering our systems, that the primary function today, I believe, as stated in the ERISA statutes, is to provide the maximum income or the maximum profit, if you will, within the system.

And from the article that I just quoted from, if I may quote from it again, it says:

> Studies based on samples of public employee pension funds nationwide show that funds with ETIs earned a return somewhere from 2 to 5 percentage points less than funds without ETIs.

I think this raises a very serious question and a very serious issue. I think we should remind ourselves exactly what the Employee Retirement Income Security Act of 1974, ERISA, says. ERISA properly codified the common law principle of fiduciary duty.

As Section 1104 says:

> A fiduciary shall discharge his duties with respect to a plan solely in the interest of participants and beneficiaries, and (A) for the exclusive purpose of providing benefits to participants and their beneficiaries and defraying reasonable expenses of administering the plan; (B) with care, skill, prudence and diligence; (C) by diversifying investments of the plan so as to minimize the risk of loss; and (D) in accordance with the documents and instruments governing the plan.

The Administration and its allies in the pension field claim that the private pension funds must be encouraged to use economically targeted investment, ETIs, that is, to do social good by encouraging investments with collateral benefits and ancillary benefits or external benefits that investment managers may not take into account under the current law.

At least that's my view.

ETIs, in other words, allegedly are a social instrument rather than an economic investment. ETIs can take a variety of forms of doing good from local job creation to environmentally green, to restrictions on investments in Northern Ireland, or whatever other may be popular at any given time.

Yet, the fundamental economic principle is that maximizing pension fund performance by each group of managers results in the best overall performance for the economy, as well as serving plan participants best.

Public pension plans have escaped the ERISA standard of fiduciary duties and they have a relatively dismal track record on economically targeted investments and so-called social investments.

Some examples include the Alaskan Public Employee and Teachers Retirement Investment in Alaskan mortgages.

The Kansas Public Employees Retirement system investment in failed home savings associations.

The State of Connecticut trust fund's investment in Colt Manufacturing Company to save 1000 jobs.

And the Missouri State Employees Retirement System failed creation of Missouri Venture Partners Program.

It is vital to the income security of our nation's millions of pension plan participants that the Federal Government's new raid on the $4 trillion in investment money be halted before it stops. Not only is their future at risk, so, too, is our children's future.

And so, I'm very pleased to be able to take part in this discussion, Madam Chair, and I look forward to the testimony of our two very distinguished guests.

SENATOR BOXER. Thank you, Congressman.

It is going to be very interesting because, right away, I can see the difference here, particularly since we have many private pension funds investing in China today.

It's very interesting. They're buying mutual funds that target infrastructure development in China.

Now, if we're so concerned about safety, which we absolutely must be, it seems to me that we should be a little more confident in what we do in America than what is going on in China.

All you have to do is look at Hong Kong. They're a little nervous. But yet, our private pension funds are investing in infrastructure in China.

So I think this whole issue is a little bit different than perhaps it once was.

So on that contentious note, I would ask Secretary Reich to begin. And also, I'm very pleased to see that we have an assistant secretary as well, Olena Berg. We're very happy to see you here.

Is it Olena or O-lena?

MS. BERG. Olena.

SENATOR BOXER. Olena Berg. Welcome, Assistant Secretary of Labor for Pension and Welfare Benefits.

Welcome, Secretary Reich and please proceed.

PANEL I

STATEMENT OF THE HONORABLE ROBERT REICH, SECRETARY, U.S. DEPARTMENT OF LABOR

MR. REICH. Thank you very much, Madam Chair, Congressman Saxton.

I appreciate the opportunity to talk about what we are doing at the Department of Labor with regard to economically targeted investments, and to highlight what American pension funds are doing in a very positive way around the country with regard to economic growth and their long-term vision of the country.

With your permission, Madam Chair, I will submit my testimony for the record and simply talk about these issues and talk about them as briefly as I can.

SENATOR BOXER. Without objection.

MR. REICH. First of all, let's be clear. The pension funds represent $4.8 trillion. That's about $3.4 trillion in the private pension area, $1.4 trillion in the public pension fund area.

We're talking about trillions.

This is 25 percent of the market value of all stocks in the New York Stock Exchange. This is one-fifth of all financial assets in the United States.

Now, it's also the case that because of their size, pension funds have a unique and very special stake in the long-term economic growth of the country. They have, in a sense, a custodial role in terms of that long-term growth. It's very difficult for many of them to beat the market because, after all, they, in many senses, are the market.

Also, if economic growth proceeds and the entire economy progresses forward, given their size and given the breadth of their portfolios, they are going to benefit.

And finally, let me stress this.

Those portfolios, the funds themselves, represent the earnings of American workers. To the extent that the entire economy is doing better, American workers have higher earnings, and that in turn creates more secure and better retirement income.

So in all these respects, pension funds, given their size and dominance in the economy, have a natural incentive to be concerned about the larger economic picture. They have a natural and unique position with regard to the national economy.

What we're questioning today, and the issue before us, is whether they are permitted, and to what extent they are permitted, to take into consideration some of these larger economic consequences.

Today, the Department of Labor is issuing an interpretative bulletin which makes very clear what the policy is, but also what the policy has been.

Congressman Saxton, this does not represent any change in Labor Department policy at all, but it does clarify the policy. And there has been some confusion about this and I think the little colloquy between you and Senator Boxer, if I may, does represent some of that confusion.

Under ERISA, it is not permissible for pension funds to engage in what might be called "social investing," to the extent that they are sacrificing risk-adjusted rate of return that they could otherwise be getting for the sake of some social good. That is not permissible under ERISA, and I'm talking now about private pension funds.

Under the law, the first and foremost obligation of private pension plans is to invest on behalf of their beneficiaries. And to meet this obligation, they must seek an investment somewhere on that frontier of risk-adjusted rate of return.

But having stated that, let me state another proposition which is equally true and which has been the policy. We are simply stating it to clarify the policy.

Even though social investing is not permitted, and it is not permissible to depart from the risk-adjusted rate of return available from comparable investments, it is entirely permissible to choose, from among those investments offering maximum risk-adjusted rates of return, one which has collateral benefits to the economy generally.

This is not a departure from previous policy. This is not a departure from the primary obligation of pension fund fiduciaries to enhance the value of those portfolios and to guard the pensions of their plan beneficiaries.

But if they can find comparable, alternative, prudent investments with similar levels of risk and return, which, at the same time enhance the economy overall, given their natural interest in doing so, and given the fact that such ancillary investments, if they are prudent, do lift the economy generally and improve the performance of the pension fund overall, that is permissible.

Not only is it permissible, but I may add, I, for one, think they ought to do it. It is encouraged. Given the $4.8 trillion held by pension funds, these kinds of economically targeted investments, as distinct from social investments, are precisely the kinds of investments that pension funds ought to be seeking.

What we are doing today, and let me be very clear about this, what we are doing today with regard to this interpretive bulletin is making clear what the policy has always been. As long as they are the equal of alternative, prudent investments in terms of levels of risk and return, it is entirely permissible for private pension funds to seek out economically targeted investments that have collateral benefits to the economy overall.

We want to eliminate the confusion. We want to eliminate the confusion because by doing so, hopefully, we will encourage more of this.

It's in the interest of beneficiaries indirectly. It's in the interest of the country, overall, indirectly.

Economists are fond of using the term, externality. Externalities simply mean benefits that extend beyond the benefits to individual investors.

The economy of the United States is filled with such so-called externalities, external benefits. We see this with regard to affordable housing. We see this with regard to infrastructure. We see this with regard to investments in people in a variety of ways. Such investments can have a very positive effect on the economy overall.

Madam Chair, you cited several examples of proper ETIs. In my testimony, I include several other examples. The Equitable Company, for example, has used its financial expertise to design real estate investments for pension funds in Boston and in St. Louis that produce strong returns for investors through renovating and constructing affordable housing.

What we've seen again and again around the country is that affordable housing can be a very, very good investment.

It is an investment which is a good investment and meets fiduciary obligations with regard to step one—that is, the minimal threshold. You must be investing at that rate which provides a return comparable to alternative prudent investments with similar levels of risk, but also includes a collateral economic benefit.

In fact, for years, because of the interpretive bulletins, it has become clear to private pensions that they may invest in venture capital. In Massachusetts, more than 100 public-sector funds have shown that venture capital investments in start-up companies can be a boon to the state's economy and, I might add, to their own portfolios.

Such investments have created some 5,000 jobs recently in Massachusetts and an average rate of return of 16 percent.

We include, again, many, many additional examples. Olena Berg, Assistant Secretary of Labor for Welfare Benefits, who has led the initiative on this, will be talking about other examples. She will also highlight an initiative that we are taking in addition to the interpretive bulletin, which I think is very important.

We're taking steps to establish an information clearinghouse for economically-targeted investments, in order to collect information and to help standardize performance data so as to assist the investment community in their evaluation.

We want to showcase past successes so that it is easier for the investment community to make these kinds of investments.

I think it's a very, very important step forward.

In conclusion, let me point out one other aspect of both the strength and also the incentives operating on investment funds and pension funds.

Pension funds are stewards of the nation's economic future in another way, beyond economically-targeted investments.

Last week, CalPERS, the $80 billion California State Pension Fund, announced that it would be considering work force policies, how employers are dealing with employees, as one of its criteria for measuring the performance of the companies that it invests in.

In making the decision, CalPERS referred to a report done independently for CalPERS on high-performance work places, and the relationship between good employer practices and the bottom line.

What CalPERS discovered and what the researchers have discovered is something that we, in doing a literature survey of the research on these areas, have also discovered. And that is, it makes sense for employers to train their employees and to bring their employees into a participative relationship on the work floor.

It makes sense for employers to be good employers of their employees because, over the long term, it shows up on the bottom line.

I bring up this example to underscore that pension funds have a unique, long-term vision. Because they cannot easily get in and out of shares of stock without affecting stock prices, many pension funds have taken a responsibility for what might be called relationship investing; that is, taking an ongoing concern with the performance of the companies they invest in.

Indeed, and just let me end on this note, because of their unique position in the American economy, pension funds can be, and are becoming, the stewards of the nation's economic future. Whether we're talking about economically targeted investments or relationship investing, pension funds take a unique view of the long-term interests of a company and its shareholders, such as the relationship between good employment practices and the bottom line. Pension funds already are making major, major contributions to the long-term health of the economy.

What we are doing today in our interpretive bulletin, what we are doing with regard to establishing the information clearinghouse on ETIs, is to encourage pension funds to move even further in the very positive direction they have already moved in.

And I just want to underscore for the purposes of Congressman Saxton and the remark you made, that the first and primary purpose obviously is the beneficiaries. Pension funds cannot depart from this standard. They cannot subordinate those interests.

But they can simultaneously consider, and should, in my view, consider a variety of ancillary consequences of the economy. This is the purpose of our bulletin.

They are large enough. They have an interest in doing so. And they are permitted to do so in our interpretation of ERISA.

Thank you.

[The prepared statement of the Honorable Mr. Reich starts on p. 48 of the Submissions for the Record:]

SENATOR BOXER. Thank you, Mr. Secretary.

Olena Berg, Assistant Secretary of Labor for Pension and Welfare Benefits, heads the agency most responsible for ERISA enforcement and, more generally, for coordinating the Administration's overall pension policy.

I'm very proud to say that she has been Deputy Treasurer of California under Kathleen Brown, who is the Democratic candidate for governor there, and that she has practical experience with ETIs and private-sector experience as a real estate investment manager. And she's a graduate of Harvard Business School.

So, with that, we are very pleased that you are here, Madam Assistant Secretary. Will you proceed, please?

STATEMENT OF THE HONORABLE OLENA BERG, ASSISTANT SECRETARY OF LABOR FOR PENSION AND WELFARE BENEFITS

MS. BERG. Thank you, Madam Chair, and Congressman Saxton. I, too, appreciate your obvious and very vociferous interest in this issue.

What I'd like to do is just say simply what we're working on in the Department of Labor as an overall policy. And that is, we're working toward a day when economically-targeted investing will be a rather unremarkable, ordinary investment practice.

Secretary Reich alluded earlier to the example of venture capital. One of the remarkable things about ERISA as a statute has been its flexibility because it doesn't prescribe specific investment policies. And that has made it adaptable over the 20 years that it's been in existence.

Roughly ten years ago, very much the same kind of debate that we're sitting here having today occurred over the appropriateness of venture capital as an investment opportunity for pension plans, with some of the very same issues—such as infusion of capital to spur economic growth, especially in underserved areas of the economy.

The Department at that time made it clear that venture capital funds, properly structured, were permissible investments under ERISA. In those ten years since that interpretation by the department, we've seen very positive results, not only for venture capital and growth of companies in the United States, but also for pension plan participants and beneficiaries.

We're saying now that there's even a broader spectrum of investments where the same is true.

Again, I'll just submit my testimony for the record, as well, to save your time, but I do want to underscore a couple of things that the Secretary said.

One was I would like to claim that I'm breaking new ground here today. But, indeed, this has been the long-standing policy of the department under both Republican and Democratic administrations.

Let me give you a couple of examples from pronouncements by my predecessors on this issue over the years.

The first one is from 1982. We said at that point:

> The protection of retirement income is, and must continue to be, the overriding social objective governing the investment of plan assets. The Department has taken the position that fiduciary considerations such as investment performance may not properly be sacrificed in order to advance the social welfare of a group or region. However, an investment is not impermissible under ERISA solely because it has social utility.

In 1991, my predecessor said:

> Since the enactment of ERISA in 1974, the department has consistently stated its position that ERISA's rules are flexible enough to permit plans to invest in areas of the economy that are most appropriate for each individual plan's circumstances.

In fact, our regulations defining the statute's prudence standard adopted a broad interpretation of that term precisely for the purpose of encouraging plan fiduciaries to look beyond traditional types of trust investments.

So the action that we're taking today is to clarify and consolidate the Department's statements of position into one document that trustees, attorneys, and others in the pension community can easily access to see exactly what the department's position is.

Now, why are we doing that?

Because there does still seem to be a great deal of confusion in the investment community about the department's position.

A couple of examples of that. Last summer, the Institute on Fiduciary Education did a survey of 119 of the largest public pension plans. They asked, are you doing economically-targeted investing? And if you're not, why not?

And what they found was that over half replied that to do so would conflict with their fiduciary duty.

There is confusion.

Similarly, the ERISA Advisory Council, when they looked at this issue last year, concluded that, in spite of the department's many pronouncements on this issue, there was a chilling effect in the private pension plan community, a fear that the department would not receive this kind of investing well.

So we recognize that we needed to be on the record on this issue and that is what we have tried to do with our interpretive bulletin.

Now, Senator Boxer, both you and the Secretary have named some successful examples of economically targeted investments. I have several more in my testimony that I recognize as well. And again, from my own personal experience, working with CalSTRS and CalPERS in California, I know you can find investments that have collateral benefits that achieve superior rates of return and do meet the goals that we're talking about here.

In fact, I'm very pleased that Dr. Bill Crist from CalPERS will be here to talk to you about those in greater detail.

The examples abound. Our contribution to the debate is to make it clear that this kind of investment certainly can be done if properly structured, as the Secretary has noted, without any violation of ERISA.

Thank you very much.

[The prepared statement of the Honorable Ms. Berg starts on p. 52 of the Submissions for the Record:]

SENATOR BOXER. Thank you very much.

To either of you, is there anything in your interpretive bulletin that would force pension funds to do anything that they're not doing now in relation to ETIs?

MR. REICH. No, absolutely not. This, again, is an interpretive bulletin that clarifies and codifies what has been the policy.

It, hopefully, through clarifying, will permit pension funds to engage in economically-targeted investments. Again, I want to emphasize, because every investment necessarily causes a plan to forego other investment opportunities, that an investment will not be prudent if it would provide a plan with a lower expected rate of return than available alternative investments with comparable degrees of risk, or if it is riskier than alternative available investments with comparable rates of return. It explicitly allows, so long as that condition is met, pension funds to consider collateral benefits to the economy as a whole. And by making all of this very explicit, by clearing away the confusion, hopefully it will encourage more economically targeted investments.

SENATOR BOXER. The reason I ask that question is, I realize that there was nothing in there to force them. But I think there's a misconception implied in my colleague's opening statement and other colleagues from the other side of the aisle, who I've heard speak on this, that this is an attempt to force some kind of an investing when, in fact, it's essentially government stepping out of the way, getting off the backs of investors and saying, look, this is a whole new area; that as long as you're prudent, as long as you go by the rate of return rule and prudence and risk and you know what you're doing, and it's as good as any other, it also has some collateral benefits.

That's why I like it, because I view it as government stepping out of the way.

I come from, again, being a stockbroker, where when you help someone invest their money, the one thing you want is the greatest array of choices to meet their needs.

So that's why I think this is such a positive step and a positive message, this interpretive bulletin and this clarification.

I also want to ask you a little bit about the clearinghouse. I'm a big fan of clearinghouses that make things simple. And I know, Mr. Secretary, you are as well.

We were able to work with this Administration and set up a clearinghouse for defense conversion where union people can call, local mayors can call, unemployed workers can call; anyone can call to find out what are the success stories of defense conversion. And happily, we're beginning to see those emerge as a result of this Administration's work in that arena.

So I would like you to go into a little bit more depth because there may be people here or others who would like to phone.

Is it set up? When will it be set up? What will people be able to access?

Ms. Berg, perhaps you.

MS. BERG. Certainly. I'd be glad to do that.

The idea with the clearinghouse is exactly what you've described, because one of the issues with economically-targeted investing are the costs, if you will, of education and the transaction costs associated with unfamiliar types of investment and setting that up.

So this is a way of getting information out to trustees who might be interested in this kind of investing, to share the success stories, to help people know who to contact and how to design things.

Now, we did not feel that it was an appropriate role for our agency to undertake, given that we're the regulators of these investments. Therefor, what we propose to do is to provide the seed financing to allow an outside, nongovernmental, nonprofit or other entity to undertake this.

We've issued a request for proposals. We'll provide the funding for the first couple of years. We'll evaluate the proposals on their ability to become self-funding after that.

84-047 O - 94 - 2

And what the clearinghouse will do is provide that kind of information: A listing of ETIs by type of investment, by geographic area, and by type of collateral benefit; information on how you can go about trying to examine the corollary benefits and evaluate the performance of these investments.

SENATOR BOXER. When do you hope to have it up and running?

MS. BERG. We hope to have it up and running by the end of the year.

SENATOR BOXER. Okay. Congressman Saxton?

REPRESENTATIVE SAXTON. Thank you, Madam Chair. And thank you both for your very eloquent statements.

I have a few questions.

The interpretive bulletin that we make reference to, I haven't seen that yet. Is that a public document?

MR. REICH. Yes. In fact, we just have it fresh off the press. It is even warm in my hands. And Congressman, you may in fact be literally the first to read the official text. And Madam Chair, let me make sure you have one as well.

SENATOR BOXER. Okay.

REPRESENTATIVE SAXTON. I see. Well, I obviously am not going to have an opportunity at this moment to read through these several pages. So let me just pursue some questions with you, with regard to this document.

An interpretive bulletin, I guess by definition, would interpret some concepts and maybe some language and some statutes and some policies that you both have said already exist, and that this is intended to eliminate any confusion.

So it would seem to me that this is maybe a paper which defines the current thought as to what our policy is. Is that a fair statement?

MS. BERG. Yes.

REPRESENTATIVE SAXTON. Thank you. This interpretive bulletin or this paper of definition, how does it interpret the following language which appears in ERISA, which you both, I think, made some reference to?

It says:

> A fiduciary shall discharge his duties with respect to a plan solely in the interest of the participants and beneficiaries for the exclusive—underlined—purpose of providing benefits to participants and their beneficiaries.

Now, in your testimony, Mr. Secretary, I believe you used words that I wrote down here as closely as I could. You said, "Under ERISA, its fiduciaries' first and primary purpose"—and if that is the conceptual language that is in this paper, which I don't know because I haven't read it yet, it would seem to conflict with the word exclusive in the statute. Is that so?

MR. REICH. No. Again, this is a mere codification, Congressman, of the policies of the Department for years under Republican and Democratic Administrations.

It is very clear that a fiduciary cannot depart from the fiduciary standard in ERISA. An investment will not be prudent—and I want to emphasize this—if it provides a lower expected rate of return than available alternative investments with comparable degrees of risk or is riskier than alternative available investments with commensurate rates of return.

In other words, the pension plan fiduciary must still be at that frontier, that risk-return frontier.

The interpretive bulletin makes clear that it is permissible—among alternative investments that are at that risk-return frontier—it is permissible for a fiduciary to consider the collateral effects on the economy as a whole. And the reasoning is, I think, very, very clear. Because of the size of pension funds, $4.8 trillion—$3.4 trillion with regard to private pension funds—those pension funds and the beneficiaries of those pension funds are likely to be helped if there is also some consideration given to collateral effects on the economy as a whole, so long as the first condition is met.

REPRESENTATIVE SAXTON. Please. I hope we're not talking semantics here.

When you say, collateral consideration given to, once again, I return to the word, exclusive, in the statute. It doesn't say primary consideration, or certainly the statute in no way mentions collateral considerations. It says exclusive purpose.

MR. REICH. That's still the case, Congressman. And again, the interpretive bulletin makes it very clear that in evaluating risks and returns, the fiduciary has got to act for the exclusive purposes and cannot sacrifice for any social good or social benefit what would otherwise be on that risk-return frontier.

The first and primary responsibility—in fact, the responsibility—is to be at that risk-return frontier.

We're simply saying that it is permissible to consider collateral economic benefits if you are already at that frontier. If you're already getting a rate of return comparable to what any alternative prudent investment with similar levels of risk would offer, it is entirely permissible to consider collateral effects.

MS. BERG. Congressman, if I might just add to that. You have focused in on exactly the legal point that has resulted in this stream of letters and requests for advisory opinions that the Department has gotten over the years. It was just exactly that point.

The statute says exclusive benefit. Does this mean that we cannot consider these other possible advantages of investments, even assuming that we can get the same risk-adjusted rate of return?

And the Department, again, in letter after letter, advisory opinion after advisory opinion, has said no, that's not what the statute means.

Exclusive purpose under the law means that you cannot weigh those things against the return. But as long as you perform your obligation as a fiduciary to get that return, it's perfectly appropriate to take into consideration those other things.

So the question that you have focused in on has been exactly the point of confusion that we're trying to, again, clarify.

Representative Saxton. So the interpretive statement, then, I take it, has in it by way of definition a statement that says, yes, it is our official policy. And you say that it has been our official policy that it's okay to make investments in these other areas and taking into consideration other economic benefits that may be derived from those investments.

Ms. Berg. As long as a fiduciary performed that initial evaluation of the investment just as an investment, and found that it offers returns commensurate with other alternative investments of equal risk.

You can't weigh one against the other.

Representative Saxton. Let me ask you this, then.

With regard to the article that I made reference to before by Marr, Nofzinger, and Tribble, do you take issue with the statement that they make here, or how do you square the logic of the statements that you just referred to in this paragraph, when it says—and I know that this may not be conclusive, but it certainly gives us some notion of some concern here:

> Studies based on samples of public employee pension funds nationwide show that funds with ETIs earned returns anywhere from 2 to 5 percentage points less than funds without ETIs.

Ms. Berg. They may have done some separate work, but there was some work done by a researcher, Olivia Mitchell, almost a year ago, which was published. And there were, first of all, some methodological problems with her calculations.

But beyond that, there aren't any pension funds—even the largest and most sophisticated—who are investing now in ETIs anywhere near the amounts that could drive those kinds of changes in return.

What you have are other things going on at the same time. I am familiar with this because, again, I was pretty actively involved in pension fund investment over the period of time that that study covers.

The larger funds that more typically do investment ETIs were also leaders in doing some things like investing internationally, investing in real estate and in other new asset categories, because as an investment manager, what you're trying to get is diversification of your portfolio. Over time, that's the best strategy.

During the short time period that the study measured larger funds and that also invested in ETIs, they tended to be more heavily invested in real estate and international investment that weren't performing so well.

So their poor performance had nothing to do with ETIs, per se.

Representative Saxton. Give us, if you will, some examples of ETIs that are going to be referred to in the clearinghouse.

Ms. Berg. Well, I can offer all the ones that Senator Boxer mentioned this morning, and those noted by Secretary Reich, and there is a list of examples in my testimony. The clearinghouse will just be an opportunity to go out and see what has been done.

And I want to stress one thing about the clearinghouse, too. It will not be a substitute for an individual plan's due diligence. And that will be made clear from the start.

This is a place to go get information if you want to find other plans to talk to, fund managers, and things like that.

But there will not be a review leading to any clearinghouse imprimatur on these investments at all. Every trustee has a fiduciary duty to examine any investment extremely carefully and make their own decision on its merits. The clearinghouse will not in any way substitute for that process.

REPRESENTATIVE SAXTON. Are there any other ways that the Department will encourage pension plans to participate in investing in ETIs?

MS. BERG. The IB and the clearinghouse were the two specific initiatives that we undertook at this time. I do go and speak to pension fund trustees about this issue in the hopes of clarifying what the department's position is.

REPRESENTATIVE SAXTON. Will there be any form of limitation put on the percentage of pension plans to be invested in ETIs?

MS. BERG. The IB points out that there is a limiting principle inherent in ERISA's fiduciary requirements. One of those standards is appropriate diversification, which means not putting too many of your assets in any asset category, whether it be ETIs, or a bond fund, or anything else that you might choose to invest in.

REPRESENTATIVE SAXTON. Well, I'm not going to pursue this further at this time, although I'll be very interested in reading the interpretive statement.

I think that you and Senator Boxer have each made reference to concerns that I certainly have with regard to encouraging investment, with an objective or objectives that include more than is specifically stated in ERISA. And I think it's fair to make that interpretation with regard to the definition that you have given this language, apparently, in the interpretive statement that you've given.

And, of course, my reasons for concern are that we have a history of federal interpretations and regulations that don't always work as we expect those interpretations might work.

Our regulation of the savings and loan industry and broad rules that permitted certain things to happen which didn't work out right, is just one example of why I think that we need to be concerned about great diversification of this kind and taking other factors into consideration, especially when at least some evidence shows that ETI-invested funds produce less investment return than non-ETI investment funds.

And so, I think those are cause for concern, and I hope, along with you, that these funds can be used productively, not only for the benefit, as the statute states, of pension participants and their beneficiaries, I hope along with you, that it works to the benefit of our entire economic system and all the participants in our economic system.

However, I think we all know that that was not the primary purpose or the stated purpose of the way we interpreted statutorily, in my view at least, the purpose of pension funds and, as a result, ancillary details that we're talking about here.

So, Madam Chair, I thank you very kindly for your permitting me to go on with this line of questioning.

SENATOR BOXER. Certainly. I would like to state that in the S&L issue, we had a failure to oversee. This couldn't be further from what we're talking about today.

I also would like to point out in these letters, which have been referred to in the interpretive bulletin, that it is very important to note that there were 15 letters noted that talked about the permissibility of considering collateral effects of an investment, as long as you don't forget your first responsibility. And 14 of those 15 letters were written by Bush Administration and Reagan Administration people.

So, certainly, I believe that what we see here is a consistency, as was stated by the panelists, to allow pension funds the ability to make the very, very best investments they can and not to preclude them from one particular area because of confusion.

So I do appreciate the fact that my colleague was here. I think sometimes, in disagreement, you get some enlightenment. And I certainly think that he did add that to this discussion, at least for me, maybe not for him.

I'm going to wrap up this panel because Secretary Cisneros is here with a very tight timeframe.

Once again, thank you very much, Mr. Secretary, and Assistant Secretary Berg, for being with us today.

Thank you.

MS. BERG. Thank you.

MR. REICH. Thank you.

SENATOR BOXER. We will ask Secretary Cisneros to approach.

Welcome, Mr. Secretary. We're very, very pleased to have you. We've just had some illuminating testimony from the Department of Labor. I think that Congressman Saxton and I were able to ask a number of questions that shed some light on the issue of ETIs. I know that you're a pioneer in this regard. So we look forward to your testimony. We know that you're on a tight schedule. We are as well, so we will move forward.

Please go ahead.

PANEL II

STATEMENT OF THE HONORABLE HENRY CISNEROS, SECRETARY, U.S. DEPARTMENT OF HOUSING AND URBAN DEVELOPMENT

MR. CISNEROS. Madam Chair, Congressman, it's well known that the Joint Economic Committee is concerned with creating stronger economic growth in our country and achieving full employment with price stability for all our citizens.

One of the best tools to ensure genuine economic opportunity for every community, every state, and every family is by generating profitable investment outlets for pension funds and other institutional investors that expand the supply of capital to meet targeted demand.

This approach, by relying more heavily on private capital markets, leverages resources that make it easier to reduce the federal budget deficit and still accomplish key goals. It brings market discipline and entrepreneurial judgment to community investment and development, establishing new partnerships based on an entirely new way of doing business by the government.

It's an essential part of the change we're trying to make at HUD.

I'm firmly convinced that the right balance can be attained by investing in affordable housing and community development. Affordable housing and community investments can be made safe and attractive for even the most careful of pension fund investors.

New York City employees retirement system funds have been leaders in community investment. They have invested in over 15,000 affordable housing units and, in the process, have earned a compound annualized return of 13.6 percent, compared to 10.8 percent yield on the fund's total fixed-income portfolio.

Another example is Pennsylvania, where the state invested $788 million in a variety of activities, including the financing of students' college educations. These investments have reached 63 basis points higher than the Donohue Money Market Short-Term Investment Benchmark in 1992.

And in California, I know that in the previous testimony, reference was made to CalPERS financing affordable single-family housing. And I know that Assistant Secretary Olena Berg worked in the California environment on this initiative.

CalPERS's projected rate of return after fees is 19.6 percent, in the process of producing affordable housing and early yields have exceeded even that rate.

We at HUD have begun looking around for additional capital sources, making it clear that pension funds, foundations, universities, religious endowments and others can participate in building their communities, even as they benefit their funds financially.

Pension funds, as you know, are an immense resource, $4.6 trillion, in the Nation.

Today, let me describe three initiatives that we have underway at HUD, which will have the effect of involving the capital markets in new and innovative ways.

Last year, Congress authorized the use of Section 8 certificates and vouchers in a community investment demonstration. The AFL-CIO Housing Investment Trust helped conceive the idea based on their experience in producing affordable multifamily housing.

The basic idea is very simple.

HUD would make available to pension funds, on a competitive basis, Section 8 project-based rental assistance to support the construction and rehabilitation of affordable, multifamily housing.

That subsidy would reduce the risk to an owner of a development by assuring that the government stood behind a portion of the units and that the full faith and credit resources of the government would pay the rent, therefore making that project financeable.

Once that was assured, that the financing was sound, that the project was financially viable, a pension fund could invest knowing that (A) its funds were safe and (B) that the returns would be competitive.

Standing behind this project is Fannie Mae, which, in short order, buys out the pension fund, assuring that they are completely safe in terms of their resources and, yet, the project has benefited from that initial infusion of new capital.

That $100 million which Congress authorized last year will leverage $1.2 billion worth of housing product, convert that into 12,000 housing units and 15,000 jobs.

Now, the application process for that $100 million is still open. But we've already received applications from the California Public Employees Retirement System, working with a group called BRIDGE Housing Corporation.

You're familiar with Don Turner's work out there, Senator, and it is truly phenomenal.

Senator Boxer. Yes.

Mr. Cisneros. The Board of Pensions and Retirement of the City of Philadelphia, working with the Philadelphia Redevelopment Authority; the New York City Comptroller's Office, on behalf of the New York City Employees Retirement System, the police pension fund and the teachers retirement system; Equitable Real Estate Investment Management, representing specially targeted investment funds, community works fund; the California Community Mortgage Fund, with pension fund investors ranging from the St. Louis Carpenters to CalPERS to the Los Angeles fire and police department to the Massachusetts Bay Transit Authority. We are attracting pension fund investment in housing on a scale that has never been before, with $100 million worth of federal spur.

The CalPERS application is a reflection of the sea change that is beginning to take place among pension funds as awareness grows of good business opportunities based on meeting key economic and social needs.

CalPERS is one of the investors in the bridge initiative, along with World Savings, the California State Teachers Retirement System, the Bank of America, Wells Fargo Bank, and the Ford Foundation.

Together, they're committing more than $300 million in financing for the BRIDGE Housing Corporation, the Nation's largest nonprofit developer of affordable housing.

BRIDGE will use the funds to build 5,000 homes for low- and moderate-income residents in northern California over the next three years.

The pension funds are making construction loans to get these rental and home ownership developments built throughout the state.

HUD is currently expecting to receive numerous additional applications for this program from the AFL-CIO housing investment trust.

The trust solicited project proposals, and you will hear in a few moments from Steve Coyle, who is the single person most responsible for originating this concept. The trust received applications to package investments for its own applications to HUD, 191 proposals to build or rehabilitate over 21,000 affordable housing units. More than half of them will be for Section 8 tenants.

The proposals come from 34 states, 110 cities, from all across the country.

This demonstration with $100 million is already generating so much competitive interest from pension funds that it will clearly produce many thousands of affordable housing units, leveraging the Section 8 vouchers, safeguarding the investments of the pension funds, involving Fannie Mae that further will make the pension fund investments secure, and generating the jobs and the economic momentum that I've described.

As a result of this first-year success and the Congress's tremendous efforts to work with us in designating this first $100 million, we're asking for $400 million in authorization and appropriation in fiscal year 1995. We believe that that will be successful. It is in the authorizing mark—our 1994 housing bill both on the House and the Senate side at this point done—awaiting action in both houses. And the appropriations process is going forward.

So this initiative, which brings pension money to this kind of housing, is going well.

The second initiative that I'll speak to briefly is slightly different.

Beginning next year, HUD will sell at auction a major portion of its $8 billion portfolio of multifamily mortgages. The mortgages were originally private loans insured by FHA, but are now owned by the department.

As real estate markets began declining in the 1980s, HUD faced the same problems as commercial banks, insurance companies, and other financial institutions.

Approximately $750 million of the FHA mortgage portfolio is secured by properties receiving government subsidies, but not enough to qualify as completely subsidized properties.

Many of them are mixed-income apartment projects still in good shape that could benefit from mortgage servicing by experienced private-sector institutions.

HUD would prefer that such institutions are long-term investors, sensitive to the preservation of these properties as decent, affordable housing.

A good way to accomplish this objective is through joint venture sales to pension funds of these assets. Targeted sales of these mortgages can provide a sound market investment for pension funds to deliver the appropriate servicing and management.

This summer, we will meet with leaders in the pension fund community to discuss potential market interest in purchasing our loan portfolio. We seek to do business with pension funds wanting to expand their capacity and expertise and to engage in profitable, long-term investments in affordable housing.

Based on our initial research, we're extremely optimistic about the prospects for this project. Completing a targeted mortgage sale to pension funds in 1995 will streamline the government's effort, get us out of a business that we ought not be in, which is managing properties, and ensure stable servicing for that $750 million portfolio of low- and moderate-income multifamily housing.

The third and final point that I want to address is the use of the Section 108 program to securitize community development block grant loans.

With the help of Congress, notably a California Congresswoman, Maxine Waters, who has taken a particular interest in this, HUD has revived and strengthened the Section 108 loan guarantee program. It's a program that enables state and local governments that are entitled by formula to receive CDBG grants, to borrow in the capital markets, with HUD providing loan guarantees backed by the collateral of future CDBG allocations.

The funds can then be used for economic and business development, infrastructure improvement, affordable housing and job creation in communities.

Recently, HUD established the economic development initiative to encourage local communities to leverage private capital using these 108 loan guarantees. ETI provides competitive grants for the users to help bring down interest costs and establish loan reserves for debt repayment.

Pension funds and other institutional investors are now beginning to provide financing for these Section 108 projects.

In Worcester, Massachusetts, the AFL-CIO Building Investment Trust acted as the lender on a biotechnology research facility using the 108 loan guarantees.

In Los Angeles, two new office buildings are being constructed in South Central as a result of this effort.

In Boston, Fidelity Investments, the largest mutual fund in the United States with more than $200 billion in assets, has invested $26 million in equity capital in the new World Trade Center's hotel and garage using this program.

In April, the State of South Carolina's Jobs and Economic Development Authority securitized the future income stream of loan repayments from a CDBG-funded small business revolving loan program and sold the first lien security to the MacArthur Foundation for $7.4 million.

So we have foundations becoming involved now.

The MacArthur Foundation obtained a safe and competitive return for an economically targeted investment in local economic development, and South Carolina received an immediate infusion of funds to invest in community revitalization.

One point to emphasize about this MacArthur Foundation opportunity in South Carolina is that there are other types of investors, not just pension funds, that can be drawn to affordable housing.

The Council on Foundations estimates that philanthropic foundations have a total investment portfolio of $163 billion. Now, this doesn't compare with the $4.6 trillion in pension funds. But even if a small portion of foundation endowment funds were invested in community improvements, it is substantial money from another source.

Many foundations do engage in program-related investments. But the MacArthur Foundation's purchase of economic development loan securities helps open up a potentially broader market for community-oriented capital.

University endowment funds, particularly universities that want to invest in housing immediately surrounding the university setting, hospital endowment funds that intend to stay in a central city area and want to shore up the neighborhood around them, all of these are rich sources of capital for economically targeted investing.

And what they find, again, Senator, is that the returns are the equal or better of what they do with other investments and using the kind of securitizing and secondary market instruments that are now technologically possible, the funds are totally safeguarded. The ERISA obligations to retirees and pensioners are safeguarded.

Members of this Committee, we appreciate your taking the initiative to call this important hearing. I'm pleased, Senator, that so much of this is occurring in California. As always, California is on the cutting edge of new concepts, and certainly BRIDGE and CalPERS are an example for the rest of the country.

The task before us in the country is enormous—to create the economic conditions that lift communities and lift individuals.

To succeed in this goal will depend a great deal on fully mobilizing resources and considerable financial capital to make a dent in some of these most intractable problems.

We're now embarking on a course that will help find and encourage new sources of capital to come to the plate.

I'm very pleased that, though the subject of investing pension funds in socially beneficial projects has been in discussion for decades, and certainly for the better part of the last decade, this innovative program initiated by Steve Coyle, adopted by the Congress, and now being executed by HUD, is the first in the government where we create a subsidy match that enables pension funds to safely and profitably invest in a very important social good, and that is affordable housing.

Fifteen-thousand-plus people will benefit from this initiative with the first $100 million. It's a good way to use the government's money, to use $100 million to leverage $1.2 billion.

Reinvented government, Clintonism, whatever one wants to call it, it makes good business sense.

[The prepared statement of the Honorable Mr. Cisneros starts on p. 56 of the Submissions for the Record:]

SENATOR BOXER. Thank you very much, Mr. Secretary.

Congressman Saxton, why don't you ask the first question?

REPRESENTATIVE SAXTON. Mr. Secretary, thank you for your very informative statement.

I'd like to ask you just one question. In the closing part of your remarks, you used the term, "To encourage socially beneficial investments," as the kind of role that you see for yourself.

MR. CISNEROS. No, sir. What I said was that over the last decade, people have talked about using pension funds for socially beneficial investments, have talked about using pension funds for infrastructure, roads, docks, ports, airports, water systems and housing.

Frankly, over the years, I have had some difficulty seeing exactly how a stream of revenues would be created that would repay pension funds from things such as general infrastructure.

But in housing, where there is a renter who pays rent or a mortgage, there is a stream of revenues and then that, properly structured, can repay the fund for the investment that it makes.

While the net result may be socially beneficial—that is to say, we need affordable housing as a society and we're getting it—it is a business proposition on the part of the pension fund.

I might say that in my previous job prior to coming to government, I headed an asset management company, whose job was to invest pension resources.

SENATOR BOXER. I'm sorry. I didn't hear you. To invest in what?

MR. CISNEROS. To invest pension resources in the bond market. It was called Cisneros Asset Management Company. I also served for eight years as chairman of the Fire and Police Pension Fund in my city; as mayor, I was the statutorily assigned chairman of the pension fund.

So I understand fully the fiduciary and the sacred obligations that we have to retirees.

These kinds of initiatives fully address the fiduciary responsibilities, the ERISA obligations, and yet create some socially beneficial product.

REPRESENTATIVE SAXTON. Through HUD, then, and through your position with HUD, one of your goals, you stated in your closing statement, was to encourage socially-beneficial investments?

MR. CISNEROS. That are balanced by safety and profitability.

REPRESENTATIVE SAXTON. Okay. The answer is yes.

MR. CISNEROS. The answer is yes if you take the whole phrase together.

REPRESENTATIVE SAXTON. I'm not trying to be smart here, or trap you, or anything.

MR. CISNEROS. Yes, sir. Okay.

REPRESENTATIVE SAXTON. I just want to clarify that you did say that.

Now, I'm going to ask you to square this, which I think you're going to be able to do, with the paragraph from the interpretive statement which says:

> The fiduciary standards applicable to ETIs; that is, investments selected for the economic benefit that they confer on others, apart from their investment return to the employee benefit plan, are not different from the standards applicable to the plan's investments generally.

In other words, any social investing that we encourage, I think this says, must fit into a category of investment which would be no more risky.

MR. CISNEROS. Correct.

REPRESENTATIVE SAXTON. And no less profitable.

MR. CISNEROS. Correct.

REPRESENTATIVE SAXTON. Than any other investment that would be made pursuant to ERISA language.

MR. CISNEROS. Yes, sir. I understand the point and I certainly concur that that is an appropriate statement on the part of the Department of Labor for how to proceed on this matter.

Clearly, the first obligation must be safety and security of the pensioners' money, as well as the profitability of the return.

It ought to be no less and, if possible, more profitable than any other investment.

When, in the process, it is possible to achieve those objectives and produce these important societal objectives, then pension funds should be encouraged to do that. And that's what we believe we have done with this housing initiative.

I cited earlier in my testimony three cases—in New York and in Pennsylvania and in another instance—where the returns have been in excess of what other vehicles would have allowed.

In the case of the New York City pension funds investment in housing, a compounded annualized return of 13.6, compared to 10.8 percent on their fixed-income portion of their portfolio.

In the case of Pennsylvania, their investment in educational loans yielded 63 basis points higher than the Donohoe Money Market Short-Term Investment benchmark for that fund.

In the CalPERS investment in single-family housing, a projected rate of return after fees is 19.6 percent, and the early experience has been in excess of that, all comfortably ahead of other indices, fixed-income and other indices.

Representative Saxton. Madam Chair, if I may just ask one concluding question of the Secretary.

Senator Boxer. Certainly.

Representative Saxton. You weren't here when I asked a question similar to this earlier. But I think I heard reference in your statement to profitability of plans that make these types of investments.

There is some evidence that has been brought to my attention, and let me quote from this article, which says:

> Studies, based on samples of public employee pension funds nationwide, show that funds with ETIs return anywhere from 2 to 5 percentage points less than funds without ETIs.

Mr. Cisneros. I can't speak to that. I really can't. I have not seen that data. All I can tell you is that in the specific instances that I have cited, the highest profile and most highlighted experiences, they have produced returns that are superior.

Representative Saxton. I think you can agree that if there is evidence that shows the results that I just read from that paragraph, certainly, we, as members of the Senate and the House, would have a strong responsibility to monitor the situation to make sure that pension funds are in fact earning what they should, while being encouraged by the Department of Labor, and now HUD, to make ETI types of investments.

Mr. Cisneros. Congressman, I would say that you have a strong responsibility to monitor these in any event, and that that monitoring should be welcome on the part of pension manager. Any time something like this is done, there is always someone who doesn't get the message and embarks on practices that are off of the norm.

And so fairly narrow guidelines and narrow interpretations and monitoring and scrutiny should be part of the expectations because of the stakes of what's involved here.

Representative Saxton. Well, that's right. And as I said to the Secretary and the Assistant Secretary a few minutes ago, Senator Boxer and I in particular have lived through a situation where we thought savings and loans were being properly administered and properly monitored while investing in housing.

The results of that have taught us very serious lessons.

Mr. Cisneros. Yes, sir. I would also say that the interpretation that the Department of Labor has issued strikes me as very appropriate. They have, I think, gone to the proper lengths to state the goals of security and profitability first, and then, within that context, indicated what is allowable.

I think that's the proper way to frame this.

I would also say that, knowing that you're from New Jersey, the initial applications for both the AFL-CIO portion of our first-year demonstration, as well as the other, include a lot of interest from New Jersey housing providers to generate affordable housing.

So there's a tremendous market out there. As you know, the lack of affordable housing that can be structured to provide returns that safeguard pensioners' investments really make it imperative that we try these kinds of efforts.

Senator Boxer. Thank you, Congressman.

We're going to wrap this up so that we can move along to our third panel. I wanted to make a couple of comments, first of all.

I want to compliment you because, as you and I know, and we know each other well over the years, we went into this business of politics for a couple of reasons.

One, we're probably crazy. But, two, we want to make sure that the American family's condition is improved.

And it seems to me that when we get into a situation where we have these kinds of deficits—and we don't have to argue why they're here; we know when they happened, and we know we've turned it around—we need to leverage our investments. And I'm talking about the investments we make here in our budget every single year. You have been someone who wants to do something about homelessness, who wants the working poor to be able to have affordable housing.

I just want to say that I think it's tremendous that you've been able to reach out for creative ways to do it.

Basically, I think it could be summed up as what could be better than doing well financially by doing good? That's the bottom line.

I think your answer to Congressman Saxton, who is very rightly concerned that we not in fact expose our pensioners to any kind of risk. And he did state S&Ls.

And believe me, there's more than S&Ls that we face. We've seen the junk bonds take away people's money. We've seen S&Ls. We've seen the worst kinds of problems. Now, we have derivatives, which I hope we can make sure don't bring us down. We have to look at the risk out there.

I think that what you're doing, frankly, is very prudent, and I think you've shown the examples.

I have just one question for you. Do you think it might be productive to leverage other current subsidies or guarantee programs in this manner? I'm assuming that your agency is the one with this idea. Is that correct? Are there any other agencies doing some of this that you know of?

MR. CISNEROS. I don't know of any other agency that has a concrete initiative now underway that allows pension funds to make investments in its work.

SENATOR BOXER. Well, the first thing I would like to suggest is that when you have a chance to talk to your colleagues, there may be other ways. I thought of one myself involving the Department of Energy, for example.

There's a program called EV America. The purpose of the program is to produce electric vehicles. To be exact, 5,000.

The funding is 50 percent from the public utilities who are going to use these in their businesses for their employees—5,000 electric vehicles—and they're looking for 50 percent from the government. And 25 percent is going to come from an ARPA grant.

But it seems to me, and Secretary O'Leary is very positive about her grant, that this isn't a lot of money. This is a few million dollars in terms of the overall. But there's an example of where you're going to have a product that the utilities are going to buy. And so, there's going to be a flow of money, a stream of money. That's another example.

I would hope that you might pledge to me that you will discuss this with her and others because it allows us to leverage the investment.

I am absolutely delighted to hear your testimony. This isn't pie-in-the-sky. You have cited the examples. You have met the return on investment test; you have exceeded it.

As a matter of fact, my own view is, and I feel this way, if an investor who makes decisions for these huge pension funds passes up an investment that will yield an excellent return, as good or better as any other, but, by the way, has collateral benefits—which is what Secretary Reich talks about—then I think they would be shirking their responsibilities, because by investing in some of these programs, rather than in infrastructure in China or Japan—and we're seeing that happen increasingly—we're helping our people get jobs. We're helping the pensioners get a good investment, but also, we're putting their families to work.

So I guess I don't have a question. I guess I'm saying thank you.

MR. CISNEROS. Thank you, Senator.

SENATOR BOXER. And we really look forward to more of these success stories.

MR. CISNEROS. Senator, I've had the privilege of serving as, as I said, chairman of the Fire and Police Pension Fund in my own hometown and as a member of the Finance Committee of the Rockefeller Foundation, which oversaw the investment of the endowment of Rockefeller. And in both cases, I saw our local pension fund invest in upscale real estate that went bad, shopping malls that went bad.

I saw the Rockefeller Foundation invest in foreign stocks of emerging countries and bonds of emerging countries in bankrupt companies, and in every other kind of fancy investment scheme.

Here is something safe and profitable that affects our own communities, that creates jobs and economic prosperity, where great attention has been given to the financial soundness and ERISA obligations and so forth.

I think you're correct, totally correct, in giving it this kind of forum so that it can be interpreted that encouragement to these kinds of investments is appropriate.

SENATOR BOXER. Okay. I do actually have one question.

MR. CISNEROS. Okay.

SENATOR BOXER. Do you think it would be productive, in terms of leveraging more private investment with partnerships of this sort, to revisit systematically a wide range of existing federal subsidy and loan and guarantee programs, with an eye toward perhaps restructuring them to leverage private institutional investment?

MR. CISNEROS. Yes, Senator, I do.

First of all, the Federal Government, in an era of deficit reduction, needs to leverage its resources upward.

What we're doing with $100 million to generate $1.2 billion worth of housing product is a whole lot better than having to come up with $1.2 billion worth of government money to spend every dollar to produce a dollar's worth of housing.

Second, I do believe that many of our programs have not been—and I mean government-wide—scrutinized for this purpose, how they can be imaginatively leveraged with private capital.

Clearly, one of the hallmarks of our age must be more effective partnerships, more effective structuring of financial opportunities, and I think the government has substantial work ahead to scrutinize its programs and look at them in this way.

SENATOR BOXER. Thank you very much, Mr. Secretary. We really enjoyed hearing from you.

MR. CISNEROS. Thank you.

SENATOR BOXER. I will call our final panel: Stephen Coyle, Chief Executive Officer, AFL-CIO Housing Investment Trust; William Crist, President, Board of Administration, CalPERS, California Public Employees Retirement System; Lee Smith, Executive Director, Excelsior Capital Corporation; and William Niskanen, Chairman of the Board, the Cato Institute.

Gentlemen, welcome. I'm going to start right away because I've been told I need to be over at the Capitol at a quarter of 1:00. So we're going to move. And I would like to ask you to summarize your testimony in five minutes, if possible, and I'm going to ask Congressman Saxton to ask his questions first.

84-047 O - 94 - 3

Hopefully, if we get through this panel, we'll have a chance for Congressman Saxton. But let's go and see if we can hold your comments to five minutes.

Stephen Coyle, we welcome you and ask you to please make your statement.

PANEL III

STATEMENT OF STEPHEN COYLE, CHIEF EXECUTIVE OFFICER, AFL-CIO HOUSING INVESTMENT TRUST

MR. COYLE. Senator Boxer, Congressman Saxton, I will turn to the point of the inquiries today and submit my written testimony for the record.

SENATOR BOXER. Without objection, it will be received.

MR. COYLE. My name is Stephen Coyle. I'm the Chief Executive Officer of the AFL-CIO Housing Investment Trust.

I also chair the policy committee of the Building Investment Trust. These are two intermediaries established by the AFL-CIO to invest pension funds raised from a host of funds, some 400 across the country, in housing and economic development activities.

CalPERS, by the way, is a major investor in both trusts.

Secretary Cisneros discussed the Community Investment Demonstration Program that has been begun authorized by Congress and is now being implemented by HUD. I'd like to comment on that program briefly. And also, I'd like to talk briefly about two transactions under the 108 loan guarantee program which address Congressman Saxton's questions about security, underwriting, and what kind of economic activities can happen under that program. It is important to bring these discussions down to the transaction level so that people can understand that these investments are not speculative exercises. These transactions involve a very serious set of economic investment decisions.

Personally, I have some discomfort with our investments being put in the framework called "ETI." That aside, when we travel this country, as all of us do, we recognize the economic needs in America's communities. When we look at the condition of our economy today, and look to the future for our children and compare that to the prospects we had 20 years ago, we are troubled. Some degree of targeted investment is in order.

We see disinvestment. We see job loss. We see the distance between those who have and those who do not have widening, and we're worried about this.

We also know that these conditions occur at a time when the resources of the Federal Government are increasingly limited.

At the same time, we recognize that pension funds are growing. Their rate of growth is greater than the growth of the economy. So people naturally look to pension funds for investment capital.

What I think we should discuss is the question: Under what policy would one say investing in housing or investing in inner city retail, or research centers, or manufacturing is not part of a broader national economic policy?

To set up ETIs versus market behavior or market investment is to set up a false, dichotomous choice.

We simply hold the proposition—for anyone to scrutinize—that these kinds of investments—investments in affordable housing, urban retail, emerging economies—are necessary. They are part of making a healthy economy and a healthy society, and they can be done safely and prudently.

Let's look at one example, the Worcester Biotech Research facility. I referred to it in my written testimony.

The community of Worcester came to us after local lenders declined to invest in the development of a research center, a 93,000-square foot research and manufacturing center in the Worcester Biotech Park. A number of local and regional different banks and funds turned them down.

Why is that?

The tenancy of this facility would be largely biotech firms. At their start-up phase, they are not ratable credit tenants. They would, if you put them into a market context, be harder to underwrite.

We explained to them that by using an existing federal program, we could make about a $12 million loan to them at market rates, and by using this program as a standby declining balance letter of credit or reserve, we could protect our investment.

How did it work?

The city agreed to pledge $11.7 million of its Section 108 program funds as a standby guarantee of our investment during the construction period. Then after the initial operating period was over, a 1.0 coverage ratio was achieved.

Now, the coverage ratio was simply, as you all know, the ratio of the net income of the project to the debt service requirement.

During the term of the permanent loan, the guarantee declines from 60 percent of the loan to an irreducible 20 percent based upon performance of the venture. So as the debt coverage ratio improves from 1.0 to 1.10 to 1.20 to 1.30—with 1.30 being a market debt coverage ratio—the reserve fund declines from 60 percent to 20 percent. We hold the 20 percent guarantee for the life of the loan to deal with unforeseen events.

So let's step back. What happens at the end of this exercise? The market players take on more of the risk and the public guarantee declines and those funds are recycled.

Now, that's an existing program. About 40 or 50 of these transactions are done each year. My recommendation to this Committee is to look at the Section 108 program, expand that program. It is not a pie-in-the-sky kind of exercise. It's filling a gap that is not being filled by the market. When you fill that gap, then the market will buy that loan paper.

Another transaction, in South Central Los Angeles at 54th and Crenshaw. We're going to go into construction this summer. This is a different kind of phenomenon. There, a state lease would provide the cash flow to repay the loan. It's a 20-year lease. The developer worked with the legislature and the state officials, local officials, and the community, and developed a simpler format, a capital cost reduction to get to the right loan-to-value and the right coverage ratios. We used $1.6 million of Section 108 funds to write down the acquisition and prep costs for the site.

Let's abstract the two experiences.

It is possible to bring the transactions in the inner city or the emerging economies or biotech or medical instrument production to places where we need new jobs for the future. We can bring that into the mainstream of finance by filling the gaps that exist in those transactions by the use of the federal programs and guarantees.

The Federal Government does not finance the project. It provides a declining and leveraged guarantee. This kind of assistance can bring pension fund investors into these kinds of transactions.

Some other general observations.

SENATOR BOXER. If you could complete in one minute, that would be fine.

MR. COYLE. All right. First, we should make certain that when we talk about these kinds of transactions, we're not talking about direct investments. Much of the studies are based upon the past where people made direct investments in local transactions.

That's a mistake.

Number two, these transactions must have good, solid, secure underwriting by third-parties.

And number three, the information to be generated by the proposed ETI clearinghouse should not be general economic theories. It should be practical how-to information, how to get things done in the world of modern real estate finance.

I think this Committee, convening this kind of forum, will help us all put together the kinds of things we need to make the capital and the pension funds available to our economy in ways that are safe, in ways that are prudent.

Thank you, Madam Chair.

[The prepared statement of Mr. Coyle starts on p. 62 of the Submissions for the Record:]

SENATOR BOXER. Thank you, Mr. Coyle. That was perfect, five minutes.

Mr. Crist, it is my pleasure to welcome you here. You're the President of the Board of Administration, CalPERS, California Public Employees Retirement System. I am very proud of a lot of the things that you are doing in health care and in some of these investments, and we're delighted that you're with us.

STATEMENT OF WILLIAM CRIST, PRESIDENT, BOARD OF ADMINISTRATION, CALIFORNIA PUBLIC EMPLOYEES RETIREMENT SYSTEM (CALPERS)

MR. CRIST. Thank you, Madam Chair, and fellow Californian, and Congressman Saxton. It's my pleasure to be here today.

In addition to being president of the board, I'm also an academic economist at one of California's state universities. I apologize for the economist part. The rest I don't.

I would read to you just one brief phrase from the California constitution, Article 16. The constitution states that my Board of Administration:

> ... shall discharge their duties with respect to the system solely in the interest of, and for the exclusive purposes of providing benefits to participants and their beneficiaries, minimizing employer contributions thereto, and defraying reasonable expenses of administering the system and that the Board's duty to its participants and their beneficiaries shall take precedence over any other duty.

I want to assure the Joint Economic Committee that the Board fully understands the requirements of the California constitution and that each member of the board exercises the utmost care, skill, prudence and diligence in carrying out their fiduciary responsibilities.

As you know, we're not under ERISA, per se. Our standards are at least as high.

With this in mind, I'll share, in the brief time I have, some of the nature and focus of our policy on economically targeted investments, the extent of our commitment to such investments, and the reasons we are able to make such investments.

Some argue that ETIs are no more than social investments. That term has been used here this morning. These investments, so-called social investments, would not be made by prudent fiduciaries because they are based partially on considerations other than those in the immediate best interest of the owners of the assets.

It is clear to us at CalPERS, however, that the present and future financial health of our trust fund is inextricably related to the economic health of California.

Beyond the obvious microeconomic analysis that is required to make specific investment decisions, it is not only necessary for us as prudent fiduciaries to simultaneously consider macroeconomic conditions, it is also necessary for us to consider the macroeconomic implications of our investments.

In other words, it is not merely acceptable to consider what are referred to as the collateral economic benefits of any investment. It would be imprudent not to include such considerations in the investment decisionmaking process.

CalPERS adopted an ETI policy in April 1993. A copy of that is part of my formal written testimony.

The geographical area focused on in our policy's definition is, of course, California. The policy statement identifies ten guidelines for ETI investment, including no concession of risk and cost-adjusted return, no distortion of our established overall asset allocation and geographic diversification guidelines, and strict quarterly performance evaluation requirements based on market prices.

Our system's ETI investments are distinguished by the fact that they represent investments that are undertaken within California and not merely part of a broader investment strategy in national or international markets.

We do not consider or account for our ETIs as a separate asset class, with a specific asset allocation or a separate target rate of return.

Rather, investments that one might identify as ETIs may be made in any asset class, as long as they can be made with risk-adjusted market rate of return expectations.

There is no downgrading of investment-quality contemplated, implied, or assumed in any ETI opportunity approved by CalPERS. To do so would violate CalPERS's ETI policy and fiduciary standards.

The primary impact of CalPERS's ETI policy has been, and probably will continue to be, in three asset classes—real estate, alternative investments, and private equity.

Funds committed to ETI projects, funds leveraged into the projects and the resulting total investments are also shown in a table in part of the written testimony. You may refer to those later.

Real estate ETI investments consist of single-family housing construction, affordable housing mortgages, residential acquisition and development, financing, and commercial mortgages.

You've heard about our single-family housing program today. I'm pleased to tell you that at this point in time, we have put $633 million into that program. This is for 64 housing projects; 7,734 units have been completed or are near completion. And that creates, according to a statistic generated by the National Association of Homebuilders, about 15,000 jobs.

We also, as I said, do alternative investment and we have a special policy on that.

These investments are intended, by policy, to stimulate the California economy and promote job growth, while earning superior investment returns.

We have found such opportunities. They're out there. They're out there where capital gaps and inefficient markets exist. We can make these investments, and have. They're very profitable. We believe they're good, sound, safe investments and we'll continue to search for more.

I'm running out of time. I want to mention one of the greatest obstacles to positive state and federal government involvement that has come up today, again and again.

Past experiences with different types of so-called raids was mentioned also today, and unwarranted political pressure on some funds to make social investments have made good fiduciaries very skeptical of anything that you do in Congress to encourage this kind of activity.

I want to make it clear that we will work against any attempt by government to raid our fund using any device within imagination, and we will not agree to invest any portion of the fund in what I have chosen to call PTIs, or politically targeted investments.

I know, Senator Boxer, that's not what you're looking to do either, or you, Congressman Saxton, and neither are we.

We reject PTIs.

Demonstration programs which contain imaginative ways of attracting pension fund investment are useful, in that the experience gained will reduce the skepticism generated by other threatening approaches to obtaining needed capital.

Secretary Cisneros spoke wisely of those things today.

I'll conclude by saying that there are capital gaps. There are inefficient markets and there are demonstration programs being developed that make it very possible, which funds the size of CalPERS, with the highest standards of due-diligence and prudence, make investments which can be called ETIs.

While this hearing is very general, it's a very valuable beginning. I thank you for the opportunity to be part of this positive change.

[The prepared statement of Mr. Crist, together with attachments, starts on p. 68 of the Submissions for the Record:]

SENATOR BOXER. Thank you, Mr. Crist.

I want to call to the attention of my colleague and others, and to the press, your three-page policy statement on ETIs, which is really important to look at, dated April 19, 1993, which clearly states what I think everyone here has stated:

> CalPERS will only consider ETIs which, when judged solely on the basis of economic value, would be financially comparable to alternatively available investments.

I think, if anything, we come out of this hearing with, it's that statement, that that's what we're talking about. See, they're applauding.

[Laughter.]

SENATOR BOXER. Because, as you can tell, that's the concern that has been voiced.

I really feel the fact that you have already done this and you can know from this Senator from California, we're going to use you as an example, and not try in any way to challenge what you're doing, but, in fact, to allow you to continue what you're doing without interference.

Lee Smith, Executive Director, Excelsior Capital Corporation.

Welcome, Mr. Smith.

STATEMENT OF LEE SMITH, EXECUTIVE DIRECTOR, EXCELSIOR CAPITAL CORPORATION

MR. SMITH. Thank you. Madam Chair, Congressman Saxton, thank you for the opportunity.

With your permission, I'd like my full statement inserted in the record.

SENATOR BOXER. Without objection, so ordered.

MR. SMITH. And I'll give you an abbreviated, condensed version of it.

I'm the Executive Director of Excelsior Capital. It's a not-for-profit corporation established by the State of New York to work with public, union and corporate pension funds to develop market-based ETIs.

Now, I think it would be a little remiss for me to not point out, being from New York, that we've been doing this for over a decade. It's a fairly established and settled question in New York, the state legislature having amended its retirement law on several occasions to encourage pension funds, public funds, to make prudent investments that also help the state's economy.

We have over a billion dollars of programs that have been done. We're now trying to build on that by involving union pension funds and corporate pension funds, because we think that this obligation to think about the effect of investments is not solely a public-sector pension fund issue.

This is an obligation that every trustee has because the fact is beneficiaries have more than one interest. They have an interest in the retirement check. They also have an interest in the health of their community. They have an interest in continued employment opportunities.

It's important for trustees to understand these multiple interests and take them into account.

What distinguishes an ETI from any other investment is the focus on the economic impact. All investments have an economic impact. The difference here is that you're conscious of them and you're trying to either maximize them or capture them for the fund or the beneficiaries.

What we've been doing in New York is focusing on collaboration with the private-sector funds. We think that the barriers to ETIs are slowly coming down. I should point out that up until this point, up until very recently, this happened with little help from the Federal Government, and we're very pleased to see the action today by the Secretary and the Assistant Secretary to clarify some misconceptions that have been associated with ERISA's treatment of ETIs.

We think, however, that there are still practical impediments to the spread of this, and we think that there is still an important agenda for public officials to continue to pursue to spread the adoption of ETIs by pension funds.

Let me skip to the question of the action agenda since we don't have much time.

The clarification of ERISA is an important first step. And the reason for that is because trustees have thought that they were being held to a higher standard when they considered an ETI. When they started thinking about the collateral benefit, they thought that the Department of Labor had a presumption against that and that, somehow, they would have to prove that it was better than any other investment.

In fact, what the interpretive bulletin is saying is what has been said all along. This investment should be treated like any other investment, and that's an important first step.

I think the clearinghouse idea is a very good idea, and I'm glad to see that they're going to move ahead on that, because information about investment is critical to help trustees do it effectively.

The transaction costs—that is, the time and energy it takes to develop ETIs—is a barrier to people doing it, and the information will help.

I think, beyond that, we would be aided if the government would sponsor a fairly extensive technical assistance and education program for trustees and fund managers.

They have enormous responsibilities. If you look at the staffing patterns with most pension funds, they have very little staff in relationship to the size of their assets. They spend a lot of time being concerned about their equities and bonds and not a lot of time on ETIs.

If we had a training and technical assistance program, that would help a lot.

And finally, I would suggest, Senator, that in your capacity as an elected official from California, I think it would be worthwhile for you to spend time meeting with corporate pension funds headquartered in California, the public funds, and encouraging them to pursue this.

The major impediment here is that trustees and fiduciaries still don't think that it's their responsibility to be concerned about these things.

And I think it is and I think it can make good investment sense, and that's what the experience we've had in New York and elsewhere has shown. Thank you.

[The prepared statement of Mr. Smith starts on p. 78 of the Submissions for the Record:]

SENATOR BOXER. Thank you, MR. SMITH.

I want to compliment the panel. You've all been succinct and to the point and very helpful.

Our final witness today is Mr. William Niskanen, Chairman of the Board, the Cato Institute.

We want to welcome you here. Please proceed.

STATEMENT OF WILLIAM NISKANEN, CHAIRMAN OF THE BOARD, THE CATO INSTITUTE

MR. NISKANEN. Thank you, Senator Boxer. My written statement will be submitted for the record. Let me make some general comments.

My own sense is that the interpretive bulletin that was released this morning is either meaningless or mischievous. It's not quite clear yet.

SENATOR BOXER. Meaningless or what? What was your second word?

MR. NISKANEN. It's either meaningless or mischievous. It's meaningless if it does not change the standard that ERISA investments must meet. It is potentially mischievous if it does change the standard.

Secretary Reich has gone out of his way to say that it doesn't change the standard. But at the same time, we've heard any number of witnesses say that we ought to encourage more investment in infrastructure, in housing, in firms that invest in their own labor force, and in other politically favored groups.

There is considerable danger, I think, that whatever pressure is brought to bear will be used to change the portfolio of pension funds in a way that will jeopardize the interests of the plan participants.

The record is quite consistent in areas of the public pension programs that have been subject to considerable political pressure.

A number of studies over a ten-year period have demonstrated that the rate of return is substantially lower in plans that have these economically targeted investments than in plans that do not.

There may be situations, some of which we've heard about this morning, in which the individual investments do not have a lower yield, but the pattern is that they do have a lower yield over the whole set of investments that are made by these public employee pension plans.

You should also be clear who is the loser in these plans. It's the public employees themselves who are the loser. Either the state and local governments must put up more money to fund the same pension promises, in which case they pay lower wages, or the pension fund itself risks bankruptcy, in which case the people risk losing some of their pension benefits.

Any measure that would reduce the yield on private pension plans would have the same effect, in that the primary losers would be the plan participants themselves. And with the case of private pension plans, the Pension Benefit Guarantee Corporation also risk losses if the plans are not adequately funded and, as with the S&Ls, possibly the taxpayers are ultimately the potential loser.

So there is reason to maintain a hard line against economically targeted investments. A more accurate term, in fact, is politically targeted investments, because these investments are ones that are most unlikely to be made in the absence of political direction or pressure.

We should maintain a hard line against these investments. If you believe that some how the market has missed out on investment opportunities that yield a high yield, I encourage you to put your own money in it.

If you believe somehow that, as a Nation, we ought to put more money into certain activities than the market itself will support, I encourage you to do it through the budget, by reallocating existing expenditures, or by reducing the federal deficit.

Don't lean on private pension funds. Keep your sticky fingers off my pension fund.

Thank you.

[The prepared statement of Mr. Niskanen starts on p. 82 of the Submissions for the Record:]

SENATOR BOXER. Thank you for your remarks. And I would ask, Congressman Saxton, if you could ask your questions.

REPRESENTATIVE SAXTON. I know what I want to ask. I'm not sure I know how to put the words together to ask it, but I'm going to try anyway.

Let me start this question with a statement. And that is, from my experience in business, I have found that it is very unlikely to find two investment opportunities that are exactly alike in terms of return, exactly alike in terms of anticipated risk. And therefore, we all use our best judgment in terms of our personal portfolios on what we want to invest in, in terms of rate of return and risk.

And so, if there are no two investments that are alike, then we all have to make judgments and in terms of pension funds, the fiduciary responsibility says, you will make the best judgment you can.

So we enter into the process with what the law says, exclusive responsibility of doing that for the members of the pension fund, what have been described in other ways as primary responsibility for doing that in terms of the pension fund. And we introduce the concept of ETI, which says, hey, if everything else is equal, which it's not, if I'm right, if everything else is equal, then we'll choose investments that do some other good along the way in terms of housing, or infrastructure, or some social good.

And then somewhere along the way, we draw the line again and say, but if we go beyond certain parameters that are undefined, then we begin to make judgments based, to some degree, maybe a large degree, on what social good we do.

And I guess my question is how do we decide where the most important factors are? Or how do we decide when we've gone too far in making these judgments for economic good for everybody, or are we now making judgments that have something to do with the social responsibility that we have to society?

I don't know how you draw those lines. I've listened to this discussion this morning and obviously, it seems obvious to me anyway, that the language in the ERISA statute is very clear. And yet, we move a little bit away from that and then we say, but if we go too far, it becomes social investing and we don't want to do that.

How do we make those decisions?

Senator Boxer. Yes, Mr. Crist?

Mr. Crist. Madam Chair, may I speak to that?

There's a right and wrong way to do everything. And Congressman, you said that we think that plan participants are the primary responsibility.

At CalPERS, we don't think the primary responsibility is to the beneficiaries. It's the sole responsibility.

So we don't do it the way you suggest, where we take and try and find a bunch of investment opportunities that are otherwise the same and, as we economists say, *ceteris paribus*, then pick one that somehow does social good. We don't focus on social good.

What we do is, we consider the macroeconomic implications of our investments, which, using other language, is to take a look at what are called collateral benefits, at the same time we analyze the specific investment.

You're quite right—no two are alike.

But I submit that it is a mistake for fiduciaries not to consider what are called collateral benefits now in the literature when they make regular investments.

It has been our experience by doing it that way, and I can't speak to Alaska and Kansas. I don't chair those boards of trustees. And there are such things as bad ways of doing things. But what we do is, we consider everything at once and we've discovered that we can in fact have good investments which do provide for, by someone else's measure, what are called collateral benefits.

Senator Boxer. Okay.

Mr. Coyle. May I add a comment?

If we were to look at the $4.8 trillion of pension assets in the single-employer corporate funds, the public-sector funds, and the Taft Hartley funds, and we were to hold up what those portfolios looked like today, we would see pretty comparable distributions into bonds and corporate equities, fixed-income securities, real estate, short-term and venture capital. We'd see pretty similar patterns from those three groups. Slight differences between public funds on the bond market versus the corporate funds.

So right now, there is a pattern that already exists in the behavior of these trustees and their advisors.

Our message is that those projects or ventures or activities that are not currently mainstreamed into the investment decisions can be structured to fit them into the existing categories.

I object to the notion that we're choosing between market behavior and ETIs.

An example of what we have tried to do is a proposal for housing AIDS victims on a scattered-side basis in New Jersey. Banks have been reluctant to make that loan. However, by using Section 8 certificates as a predictable source of project cashflow, the secondary market will be able to purchase and securitize the loan to build this type of housing. Securitizing that cashflow will allow Fannie Mae to issue a mortgage-backed security, which pension funds can purchase for their portfolio.

In the final analysis, the funds that invest with the Trust are not investing in that project in New Jersey. They're investing in a national pool that's 100 percent secured. As such, these investments are just like the 11 percent of all pension assets that are invested today in secondary market securities.

REPRESENTATIVE SAXTON. Why won't the bank make the loan, then?

MR. COYLE. The bank, by making the loan directly, would own the mortgage, not a security. And absent the guarantee offered by the mortgage-backed security, they're at high risk.

So what I'm trying to say is, if people think pension funds will go to these activities without the Federal Government playing some role, that's not true. There is not a "no-cost" way of doing it.

We are saying that existing programs—be they loan guarantees, capital write-downs, or project subsidies—can be used to get better results, better leverage, better targeting, and can bring new sources of capital.

We're not recommending direct investment, high-risk investment. In the laboratory in Worcester where the banks said no, the banks didn't have a mechanism to set up a stand-by letter of credit that would decline with performance.

What we're saying to you is, don't get caught in the box called market behavior versus ETIs. That's a semantic discussion in this city. It's not what's happening out there in the world.

We're saying the reality is we need the jobs. We need to house those kinds of people. AIDS victims aren't politically preferred. That's absurd. These are people at the edge.

Nobody's coming forward to say, these people deserve the same kind of decent housing that we expect for ourselves or for our families.

So we're saying, do those things that are necessary for a healthy society and a strong economy, but do them in ways that allow the trustee to fit those activities back into their existing portfolios of pension investments.

We're not saying create a whole new category called ETIs. We're saying, if you bring the right kind of securities, and the statutes exist, you can structure these transactions to fit into those existing investment categories and it will give the same returns that one would get from investing in the bond market.

Should we pull out of the bond market because of what has happened since January in response to the Fed behavior? Should we collapse that market? Should we collapse the 7 to 10 percent of overseas investment because of the run on our currency?

Should we pull out of the stock market because returns are now down to 2½ percent?

Of course not. These are long-term cycles. We're simply saying, the needs of America's communities belong in those long-term cycles.

SENATOR BOXER. I'd like to, because we need to shut down in five minutes, direct a question at Mr. Crist.

Oh, Mr. Niskanen?

MR. NISKANEN. May I caution you against thinking that this $4 trillion is a fund for government to allocate. It doesn't belong to the government. It doesn't belong to the taxpayers. It belongs to the plan participants.

You should start with the recognition that the people who want to make investments from those funds should make a case to the funds, not to the government. The reason people are here in Washington is that they think that they can get some political help or political pressure to get money from those funds. Whereas, if they have a case to make on a rate-of-return basis, or on a local community effects basis, make the case to the fund, not here in Washington.

SENATOR BOXER. Well, I completely agree with that, that that's exactly what should be happening. And that's why I want to address my question to Mr. Crist.

You have how much in pension to invest? What's your total portfolio at CalPERS?

MR. CRIST. Our total fund, right now, is right at $80 billion.

SENATOR BOXER. Eighty billion dollars. And what percentage of that do you have in ETIs, or about how much?

MR. CRIST. What we count as ETIs, a total of $1.6 billion. So it's a very small percent, 2 percent.

SENATOR BOXER. Okay. I want to address this point of, "Keep-your-sticky-fingers-off-my-pension" remark, because I'd like to know, does anyone have sticky fingers here? Is anyone coming in and saying, you must do this, you must do that? Are they saying you must have a certain percentage of these or you shouldn't have? Is anyone under the law of California influencing your decisions, other than what you must do prudently as a trustee?

MR. CRIST. No, not in terms of investment decisions, and we would reject that. I agree with the previous speaker in that those funds belong to the beneficiaries. They belong to the members of the fund.

SENATOR BOXER. Exactly.

MR. CRIST. Absolutely no argument. There have been experiences, however, Senator, where government officials facing very difficult economic times and budget deficits, have looked at this pot of money, our $80 billion and the total $4 trillion, whatever, as a source of somehow skimming it away.

We call that raids.

What we're talking about here in ETI is not that. And we're not looking for government subsidies, in the sense of just give us some money and hold us harmless, either.

We're making sound investments. The market place is full of them. But good public/private—one thing in my written testimony that I did not get to elaborate on—good public/private partnerships, such as the CalPERS, BRIDGE, World Partnership and so on, can generate huge benefits to the economy, and thereby help those beneficiaries who own our fund.

SENATOR BOXER. I have seen governors in past, and legislators, try to raid those funds. And that is outrageous because I agree very much that what we have to do is safeguard those funds for the retirees.

They don't belong to the stock market. They don't belong to the bond market. They don't belong to ETIs. They don't belong to China, to build China's infrastructure.

Those funds and the management of those funds have to be for those people who will need to have a secure retirement.

Well, I just want to say to all of you, thank you very much for taking the time, for being so succinct, for giving us the information that we need and I think providing a forum for Congressman Saxton and I, who approach this a little bit differently, to really learn.

This hearing of the Joint Economic Committee stands adjourned.

[Whereupon, at 12;45 p.m., the Committee adjourned, subject to the call of the Chair.]

SUBMISSIONS FOR THE RECORD

PREPARED STATEMENT OF SENATOR BOXER

I want to welcome all of the witnesses and thank them for taking the time to come before this Committee to testify about the important issue of pension fund investments in affordable housing, job creation in small businesses, infrastructure and other economic development projects.

It's not an easy time for those of us who came to Washington to help create jobs and rebuild our communities. The deficit-building Reagan/Bush decade is behind us but its legacy continues to tie our hands.

The interest on the debt swallows up billions of dollars that could go to incentives for job creation and business growth, to support for new technologies, and to build a world-class infrastructure. Cutting the deficit means cutting spending—which means capital starved cities and towns across the nation will see another year go by without the funds to stimulate new businesses and new housing or to rebuild our crumbling bridges and roads.

President Clinton is moving us in the right direction. In the past two years, the President has made some critical investments in education, mass transit, job training and R&D while working to reduce our deficit. In fact, projections for 1995 show a drop in the deficit of more than 40% from earlier projections. But, investments on the scale that will drive real economic growth and build an economy that will be competitive in the 21st century are increasingly difficult.

To address these investment needs, it is clear that we need lots of creative thinking.

Today we will talk about one possible source of funds to make these necessary investments—that is "economically targeted investments," or ETIs—by our nation's public and private pension funds.

First, let me say: we are <u>not</u> talking about doing good without making money. We are <u>not</u> talking about "social investing" at below-market rates of return.

What we <u>are</u> talking about is "doing well by doing good." We are talking about investing in needy sectors of our communities while providing a real return for investors. These are `win-win" investments—investments that help our economy grow, investments that create jobs while providing solid rates of return.

We are talking about tapping the vast pension resources—which currently exceed $4 trillion—to invest in sound and profitable economic development projects.

And, most importantly, I want to say that I have not forgotten that these pension funds are the hard-earned retirement savings of millions of working Americans. There is no question that these funds <u>cannot</u> be diverted toward economic development at the expense of more profitable investment opportunities. But I do believe we <u>can</u> have it both ways. Our witnesses today are going to tell us about investments that provide a competitive rate of return while helping to build the health and productivity of our communities.

Let me give you some examples: The Boilermaker National Pension Trust has invested roughly $200 million, or about 10% of its total assets, in something called the Co-Generation Fund. This Fund is designed to target investments in electric co-generation projects—that is, projects using alternative energy sources, such as solar, geothermal, and waste, to generate electric power. The Co-Generation Fund has a projected lifetime return of over 14%—in fact, the Union considers the Fund one its best investments. This partnership is helping to create jobs for the union's workers; it is helping to create alternative sources of energy that are environmentally sound; and, it is a profitable investment for the pension funds.

And, there are other examples: in March of this year, two of California's largest pension funds—CalPERS, the California Public Employees' Retirement System, and CalSTERS, the California Teachers' Retirement System—joined a non-profit builder and three of California's biggest financial institutions to launch an affordable housing initiative. This project is expected to provide $340 million of construction loans to finance as many as 5,000 housing units in California over the next three years. This is what I call a win-win-win investment—the rate of return for the investors is competitive, new affordable housing units will be available to Californians, and the project will stimulate jobs in California's construction industry.

These kind of exciting partnerships—among pension funds and private financial institutions and industries—are what we need to stimulate economic growth and job creation and to build our communities.

ETIs by our nation's pension funds are growing in number. Laws or programs in 22 states now encourage ETIs by pension funds. But, ETIs are done almost exclusively by public and union pension funds and they represent only a fraction of total tax-exempt institutional assets. ETIs total about $25-30 billion out of more than the total of $4 trillion—that is less than 1%. In contrast, more than $150 billion in pension investments are in foreign assets outside the United States.

Finally, I want to remind everyone what is at stake in these belt- tightening times. We can not forget what these kind of investments would mean in real terms to real people in California and across the nation. ETIs could mean jobs and affordable housing and better, stronger communities.

This is an issue that is especially important to California. Defense industry cutbacks and base closures have left my great state searching for new industries and new opportunities. But we are the land of innovative thinkers. And, ETIs may be part of the answer. CalPERS is already leading the way—with a total of roughly $5.5 billion in socially beneficial and profitable investments in FY 1992.

Yes, it's not an easy time for those of us wanting to create jobs and build our communities, but, all of us here know that we do not intend to fold up our cards and drop out of the game. We intend to stay in: to fight and strategize to win.

We intend to roll up our sleeves and with the private sector, find new ways to build the new roads, airports, bridges and ports that will attract new industries and restore this nation's competitiveness. We intend to find new ways to put people to work, not on make work but on needed work, and new ways to improve the quality of our lives.

The Clinton Administration is taking an aggressive approach. Proof of the Administration's enthusiasm is the presence here today of not one, but two Cabinet secretaries—HUD Secretary Cisneros and Labor Secretary Reich.

I hope that today's hearing will answer some unanswered questions about how to put pension fund resources to work on important economic development projects: What can we in the federal government do to encourage ETIs? How do we get private pension fund investors more interested in sound and profitable ETIs? What can be done to provide pension fund managers with information about the previously unknown world of ETIs? Cam we move beyond housing to find other sectors that could benefit from ETIs? What government funds or subsidies—such as ARPA grants or empowerment zones—can be used to leverage and attract other investment money?

During today's hearing we will hear from people who are working hard to come up with ways to make these kind of investments possible. I applaud them for their work and I look forward to the testimony of all of our witnesses.

PREPARED STATEMENT OF THE HONORABLE MR. REICH

Madam Chair and Members of the Committee:

It's a pleasure to appear before the Joint Economic Committee. I commend the committee's leadership for addressing the issue of Economically Targeted Investments (ETIs). This morning, I want to share with you the Clinton Administration's views on ETIs—in particular, how our nation's pension funds can invest their dollars not only to achieve competitive rates of return, but also to generate long-term, broad-based economic benefits.

Let me be clear at the outset precisely what I mean by an economically targeted investment. An ETI is an investment that meets two stringent tests. First, the investment produces a competitive risk-adjusted rate of return. Second, above and beyond attractive returns, the investment produces collateral benefits to workers and communities in the form of infrastructure, housing, job creation, or enterprise development.

As the members know, there has been some confusion in recent years about the extent to which ETIs are consistent with a pension fund's fiduciary responsibilities. One reason for this murkiness is that ETIs are frequently confused with what is known as "social investing." In current parlance, this term usually refers to investment practices that subordinate financial return to some other social objective. The Department of Labor does not condone the use of pension funds in this manner. We prohibit it.

ETIs are <u>not</u> social investing. They are instead a way that pension funds, whose position in the American economy is uniquely powerful, can satisfy their primary responsibility by deploying their assets to lift the entire economy.

Today, in an effort to clear away any confusion that may surround this matter, the Labor Department is issuing an Interpretive Bulletin that clarifies the law and codifies our long-standing position. Our Interpretive Bulletin reaffirms what has always been true: ERISA, the federal law that governs pensions, does not prohibit economically targeted investments. Pension plan fiduciaries who invest funds in an ETI are acting well within their legal responsibilities so long as the ETI generates a competitive risk-adjusted rate of return, and so long as the ETI is an otherwise appropriate investment. If a pension fund meets its first obligation, achieving a competitive risk- adjusted rate of return, ERISA presents no barrier against efforts to produce collateral benefits for the wider economy. We will encourage funds to reach for such collateral benefits, because—far from conflicting with their fiduciary duties—doing so complements their responsibilities to plan participants.

With me this morning is Olena Berg, Assistant Secretary of Labor for Pension and Welfare Benefits, who will explain the Interpretive Bulletin in greater detail. She has been the engine behind these efforts, and has used her office and her own extraordinary talents to bring ETIs to wider attention. Our mutual hope—and I know the hope of many members of this committee—is that by dispelling some of the uncertainty about the law in this area, we can foster the wider use of ETIs.

This bulletin comes at a moment when the American economy is in the thick of historic change. International trade—and especially, new technologies—have shattered the fundamental premises of the economy our country once knew. Capital and information can now wash easily across national borders, which means a nation's key economic resources are those that remain fixed within its borders—primarily, people and infrastructure.

Although the economy has added more than three million private sector jobs since President Clinton came to office, we still have some eight million

Americans unemployed, about four million part-time workers who can't find full-time work, and millions more Americans who are outside the job market altogether. Long-term unemployment remains a persistent problem, and the income gap between well-educated and less well-educated workers widens more each year.

To address these problems, the Administration has launched a plan for economic renewal whose central goal is to build an American ethic of continuous lifelong learning—together with the institutions to give that ethic practical effect. In the last two months, the President has signed legislation to establish world-class educational and skills standards, and to ease the transition from school to work for the 75 percent of America's young people who do not graduate from college. We've also expanded the earned income tax credit to make work pay, and lift the living standards of the working poor. And in the coming months, the Administration will be hard at work reforming the health care system and turning the unemployment system into a re-employment system. (By the way, thank you again, Senator Boxer, for cosponsoring the Reemployment Act.)

An essential complement to this skill-building agenda is stepped-up investment in the enterprises where workers can deploy their skills. It is here where pension funds are in a unique position. Pension funds today comprise 25 percent of the market value of all the stocks on the New York Stock Exchange—and 32 percent of daily trading volume. One out of every five dollars of financial assets in the United States now belongs to a pension fund. In all, America's pension funds hold assets that total $4.6 trillion. Since that figure is so unfathomably large, let me put it in perspective. If $4.6 trillion worth of one-dollar bills were laid end-to-end, they would stretch a distance equal to 907 round-trip journeys from Washington, DC to the moon.

With holdings so enormous, it's difficult for pension funds to beat the market, because they are the market. The law of supply and demand runs smack into Heisenberg's uncertainty principle: the pension fund community has grown so immense that it cannot make a move without affecting the very market it seeks to outsmart. This dominance presents both danger and opportunity. Pension funds are so large that if many of them attempt simultaneously to dodge quickly in and out of positions, they risk disrupting the market and undermining their own objectives. But their size also offers pension funds both the incentive and the ability to improve the long-term prospects of the entire economy.

Pension funds are becoming perhaps the most vigilant and influential custodians of long-term corporate strategy. No longer content to remain passive investors, they are using their expertise and influence to monitor and improve the long-term performance of individual companies. As any CEO will tell you, nothing concentrates the mind so much as an inquiry from a major institutional investor about his or her company's practices.

Now, let me be clear about our Interpretive Bulletin and the policy of this Administration. The foremost responsibility of investment managers and trustees is to provide retirement income for plan participants and their dependents. And the only way to fulfill this responsibility is by uncovering the best possible investments for the exclusive benefit of plan beneficiaries. One reason pension funds have grown so large is the rigorous fiduciary standards that Congress established for private sector pension plans two decades ago as part of ERISA. This Administration sees no need for, and would oppose, modification of these proven standards.

But at the same time, the simple rate of return on funds set aside for retirement does not—in and of itself—guarantee a secure retirement income. Retirement income depends in part on the wages plan participants earn while they're in the work force. For example, workers who participate in defined benefit plans will receive retirement income based on their years of service and their salaries. Those who participate in defined contribution plans will receive retirement income based on what they set aside from their earnings. In both cases, rising incomes and robust job growth are essential in ensuring retirement security for plan participants.

Pension funds—their dollars reaching 900 times to and from the moon—are positioned like no other force in the American economy to raise incomes and spark new jobs. Just as owners of a substantial stake in a single company must take a patient, far-sighted view of their investments, pension funds, recognizing their status as the "owners" of much of the economy, can benefit most from similar long-term thinking.

Economically targeted investments are one important way to invest for the long term. Later in the hearing you'll learn about efforts CalPERS has undertaken in California. And across the country, several other examples abound.

The Equitable Company has used its financial expertise to design real estate investments for pension funds in Boston and St. Louis that produce strong returns for investors through renovating and constructing affordable housing. In Massachusetts, more than 100 public sector funds have demonstrated that venture capital investments in start-up trustees to invest prudently and for the exclusive benefit of the plans' participants. Investment in ETIs may meet ERISA's requirements so long as the investment has an expected rate of return comparable to alternative investments with similar levels of risk. And of course, investment in an ETI still has to be reasonably designed as part of the plan's portfolio to further the purposes of the plan. This means, among other things, taking into account the plan's investment policy and the need to diversify its portfolio. Under these circumstances, the fiduciary can take into account collateral benefits in choosing among equally attractive investments. I would like to be quite clear: the selection of an ETI for pension plan investment in and of itself will not trigger an ERISA violation. However, choosing an ETI, or any other investment, without regard for ERISA's fiduciary requirements may well run afoul of the law.

The Interpretive Bulletin makes clear that there is no reason to exclude ETIs from consideration as plan investments. The Interpretive Bulletin articulates that, so long as an investing plan adheres to the fiduciary duty requirements of ERISA, a plan's assets may be available to be put to work through ETIs in the name of America's pension plan participants and beneficiaries. The Interpretive Bulletin reiterates our point that ERISA does not require fiduciaries to reject a potential ETI solely because it promotes a healthy economy.

This is not to deny there are risks associated with ETIs. ETIs are visible. If an investment goes bad, there will be publicity. Also, there may be pressure to do these projects for reasons other than their attractiveness as investments. But we believe these risks can be managed, and indeed, ERISA's regulatory framework provides the guidance fiduciaries need to feel comfortable in choosing ETIs. For example, ETIs may be purchased through pooled investment vehicles in order to achieve greater diversification. In addition, plans may lower their exposure to loss by hiring investment managers who are experienced in ETIs and the asset categories associated with ETIs.

ETI CLEARINGHOUSE

The Department is also moving in other ways to make ETI investment opportunities more available. To help fiduciaries and investment managers choose appropriate ETIs, we are establishing an ETI Clearinghouse to showcase future opportunities and past successes to both public and private plans interested in developing ETIs. This proposal was strongly endorsed by the Department's ERISA Advisory Council last year.

This Clearinghouse will provide a case study listing of ETIs around the country, cross-referenced by investment category and collateral benefit. The Clearinghouse will also work to collect and standardize performance data on ETIs, in order to assist the investment community in their evaluation. We expect to have the Clearinghouse in operation by year's end.

CONCLUSION

That is what we are doing. What the Department of Labor is not doing is prescribing a new set of regulations or mandating formulas for plan fiduciaries. Our primary role, through the ETI Clearinghouse, the Interpretive Bulletin, and this forum, is to get out the good word that properly structured ETIs are perfectly permissible—and are, in fact, to be encouraged.

We believe that the investment community must seek out and create the investment opportunities that will serve participants by both earning the highest possible risk-adjusted return, and at the same time building an economy that creates the good jobs that lead to retirement security.

Thank you. I would be happy to answer any questions.

PREPARED STATEMENT OF THE HONORABLE MS. BERG

Good morning Madam Chair and members of the Committee. My name is Olena Berg. I am the Assistant Secretary of Labor for Pension and Welfare Benefits. I am pleased to appear before you to discuss the Department of Labor's views on economically targeted investing by pension funds. I too commend the Committee for its interest in pension fund investment policies.

INTRODUCTION

We at the Department of Labor are working to bring about the day when economically targeted investments, or ETIs, will be a rather unremarkable, everyday practice among institutional investors. As the Secretary has outlined, ETIs, if properly chosen, are one way of providing substantial long term benefits to the participants and beneficiaries of pension plans. Not only can a well-managed ETI provide a competitive rate of return for the investing fund, but this form of investing also serves to improve the performance of the domestic economy with its infusion of capital in growth areas that investors interested in only the short-term have often overlooked. The Employee Retirement Income Security Act of 1974 (ERISA) is flexible enough to give pension trustees the choice of adopting a strategy of trying to beat the market, or employing a strategy that recognizes the connection between the economy's growth and their funds' investment success.

HISTORICAL BACKGROUND

In addition to its strict fiduciary responsibility standards, ERISA provides great flexibility to investment managers regarding appropriate types of investment vehicles. As with ETI investment today, ten years ago similar questions were raised by plan sponsors about the appropriateness of venture capital companies. At that time the Department made clear that investment in venture capital companies could be appropriate for pension funds. Since then, capital has flowed from pension funds into this area of the economy, to the great advantage of pension participants and beneficiaries.

Similarly, we believe that ERISA's fiduciary requirements are flexible enough to encompass another non-traditional investment—Economically Targeted Investments.

Over the years, the Department has issued several advisory opinions and information letters in this area, all of which concluded that plan fiduciaries can invest in ETIs without violating ERISA's prudence and exclusive benefit rules. In 1982, for example, we said, "the protection of retirement income is, and must continue to be, the overriding social objective governing the investment of plan assets. The Department has taken the position that fiduciary considerations such as investment performance may not properly be sacrificed in order to advance the social welfare of a group or region; however, an investment is not impermissible under ERISA solely because it has social utility."

In 1991, we said, "[s]ince the enactment of ERISA in 1974, the Department has consistently stated its position that ERISA's rules are flexible enough to permit plans to invest in areas of the economy that are most appropriate for each individual plan's circumstances. In fact, our regulations [defining)...the statute's prudence standard, adopted a broad interpretation of that term precisely for the purpose of encouraging plan fiduciaries to look beyond the traditional types of trust investments."

To clarify the Department's position, we have consolidated these opinions and letters into an Interpretive Bulletin which will become a part of our regulations under ERISA.

Last year, our ERISA Advisory Council conducted a comprehensive review of pension investment in ETIs. This review recognized the important role ETIs can play in a dynamic investment strategy. The Advisory Council also concluded that private pension fund fiduciaries have been inhibited from investing in ETIs because of a misperception of the Department's interpretation of ERISA's fiduciary requirements. The Advisory Council therefore recommended first, that the Department publish guidance clarifying the appropriateness of ETIs for pension funds, and second, that an ETI clearinghouse be created to assist funds in choosing suitable investments.

THE DEPARTMENT'S PRESENT ACTION

ETIs are something we've done a lot of thinking about at the Labor Department. We have brought together representatives from the Departments of Labor, Commerce, HUD, Treasury, and the National Economic Council to develop an Administration-wide plan on ETIs. This interagency group is now charting how investment vehicles and credit enhancements can be structured to help attract pension funds and other institutional investors to ETIs.

But now the Department of Labor is moving from planning to action. Two of these actions I'd like to discuss today. First, as described above, we are issuing clear written guidance to pension plan fiduciaries regarding their responsibilities under ERISA when considering investments in ETIs. Second, we are taking steps to establish an information clearinghouse for ETIs which will collect information and help standardize performance data on ETIs around the country.

ETIS DEFINED AND IN USE

As the Secretary has described, ETIs are investments in a wide variety of asset categories that yield certain collateral benefits such as boosting the health and productivity of the U.S. economy. Examples of the collateral benefits brought about by ETIs include expanded employment opportunities, increased housing availability, improved social service facilities, and strengthened infrastructure.

One successful example of ETI investment with which I am very familiar is the experience of the State of California's CalPERS and CALSTERS Funds. CalPERS has committed $375 million (or about 0.5% of its assets) to primarily entry-level residential housing around the state and expects rates of return between 15% and 25% a year. Its first complete project in the program achieved a 44% return over the life of the construction loan.

The New York City pension funds have also been leaders in the area of ETIs. By working with the Community Preservation Corporation, the funds have invested more than $400 million since 1984, financing more than 15,000 housing units.

The State of Massachusetts developed an ETI program for their state teachers and employees retirement system to make investments that would benefit the state economy. The fund has sponsored the Middle Class American Dream Plan, which provides affordable mortgages to families who do not meet standard mortgage requirements. In 1992, $125 million was allocated to the program, allowing 900 families to acquire new homes.

Although good examples of ETIs abound, people still question whether ETIs are a legal and proper investment for private plans subject to ERISA. As was shown in the report, "Economically Targeted Investments," published by the Institute for Fiduciary Education in 1993, which surveyed 119 of the nation's largest public pension plans, even some public plans are uncertain if investment in ETIs is appropriate. The reason most frequently cited by these public plans for not investing in ETIs was the belief that doing so would conflict with their fiduciary duties. There is also extensive anecdotal evidence that private plan fiduciaries hesitate to use ETIs due to a similar concern that ETIs may fail to meet ERISA's fiduciary standards.

Yet, let me echo one point from the Secretary's remarks today: when properly constructed and maintained, ETIs do not create a conflict of interest, and will not violate the pension fund trustee or asset manager's fiduciary duties.

ERISA REQUIREMENTS: THE INTERPRETIVE BULLETIN

One of ERISA's overriding requirements is to assure that private pension funds shall be managed solely for the exclusive purpose of providing benefits to participants and beneficiaries of the plan. ERISA requires pension fund investment managers and trustees to invest prudently and for the exclusive benefit of the plans' participants. Investment in ETIs may meet ERISA's requirements so long as the investment has an expected rate of return comparable to alternative investments with similar levels of risk. And of course, investment in an ETI still has to be reasonably designed as part of the plan's portfolio to further the purposes of the plan. This means, among other things, taking into account the plan's investment policy and the need to diversify its portfolio. Under these circumstances, the fiduciary can take into account collateral benefits in choosing among equally attractive investments. I would like to be quite clear: the selection of an ETI for pension plan investment in and of itself will not trigger an ERISA violation. However, choosing an ETI, or any other investment, without regard for ERISA's fiduciary requirements may well run afoul of the law.

The Interpretive Bulletin makes clear that there is no reason to exclude ETIs from consideration as plan investments. The Interpretive Bulletin articulates that, so long as an investing plan adheres to the fiduciary duty requirements of ERISA, a plan's assets may be available to be put to work through ETIs in the name of America's pension plan participants and beneficiaries. The Interpretive Bulletin reiterates our point that ERISA does not require fiduciaries to reject a potential ETI solely because it promotes a healthy economy.

This is not to deny there are risks associated with ETIs. ETIs are visible. If an investment goes bad, there will be publicity. Also, there may be pressure to do these projects for reasons other than their attractiveness as investments. But we believe these risks can be managed, and indeed, ERISA's regulatory framework provides the guidance fiduciaries need to feel comfortable in choosing ETIs. For example, ETIs may be purchased through pooled investment vehicles in order to achieve greater diversification. In addition, plans may lower their exposure to loss by hiring investment managers who are experienced in ETIs and the asset categories associated with ETIs.

ETI CLEARINGHOUSE

The Department is also moving in other ways to make ETI investment opportunities more available. To help fiduciaries and investment managers choose appropriate ETIs, we are establishing an ETI Clearinghouse to showcase future opportunities and past successes to both public and private plans interested in developing ETIs. This proposal was strongly endorsed by the Department's ERISA Advisory Council last year.

This Clearinghouse will provide a case study listing of ETIs around the country, cross-referenced by investment category and collateral benefit. The Clearinghouse will also work to collect and standardize performance data on ETIs, in order to assist the investment community in their evaluation. We expect to have the Clearinghouse in operation by year's end.

CONCLUSION

That is what we are doing. What the Department of Labor is not doing is prescribing a new set of regulations or mandating formulas for plan fiduciaries. Our primary role, through the ETI Clearinghouse, the Interpretive Bulletin, and this forum, is to get out the good word that properly structured ETIs are perfectly permissible—and are, in fact, to be encouraged.

We believe that the investment community must seek out and create the investment opportunities that will serve participants by both earning the highest possible risk-adjusted return, and at the same time building an economy that creates the good jobs that lead to retirement security.

Thank you. I would be happy to answer any questions.

PREPARED STATEMENT OF THE HONORABLE MR. CISNEROS

Thank you, Chairman Mfume, Chairwoman Boxer, and members of the Committee, for the opportunity to testify to you today on such an important subject as Economically Targeted Investments and federal policy. It is well known that the Joint Economic Committee is vitally concerned with creating stronger economic growth in America and achieving full employment with price stability for all of our citizens. One of the best tools to ensure genuine economic opportunity for every community, every state, and every family, is by generating profitable investment outlets for pens ion funds and other institutional investors that expand the supply of capital to meet targeted demand.

This approach, by relying more heavily on private capital markets, leverages resources that make it easier to reduce the federal budget deficit and still accomplish key goals. It brings market discipline and entrepreneurial judgment to community investment and development, establishing new partnerships based on an entirely new way of doing business within government. It is an essential part of the profound change we are undertaking as we reinvent HUD and the other fellow agencies.

As a former asset manager myself, I understand the fiduciary responsibilities that require investment managers to strike the right balance between return and risk. I also see capital investment gaps in the areas of my current responsibilities as Secretary of Housing and Urban Development. I am firmly convinced that the right balance can be attained by investing in affordable housing and community development. Affordable housing and community investments can be made safe and attractive for even the most careful of pension fund investors.

- The New York City Employees Retirement System pension funds have been leaders in community investment. By investing through special financial intermediaries and securities such as the Community Preservation Corporation and Ginnie Mae, they've helped finance rehabilitation and construction of more than 15,000 affordable housing units, and provide mortgage financing for 4,000 low and moderate homebuyers in minority and mixed neighborhoods.

  These investments have been both beneficial to communities and profitable for the pension fund. NYCERS pension funds' $860 million in economically targeted investments have earned a compounded annualized return of 13.6 percent, compared to 10.8 percent yield on the funds' total fixed- income portfolio.

- In Pennsylvania, $788 million in state pension funds have been invested in a variety of activities benefiting the people of that state—including the financing of 77,000 students' college educations and $8.3 million worth of housing for rural families. These investments helped the fixed-income portfolio reach a yield 63 basis points higher than the Donoghue Money Market Short-Term Investment Benchmark in 1992.

- In California, the California Public Employees Retirement System—CalPERS—is financing affordable single-family housing development. CalPERS began this effort in 1992. By the end of May 1993, CalPERS had committed $375 million to finance construction of nearly 3,200 homes, representing 4 percent of all single-family housing starts in California in 1992. CalPERS projected rate of return, after fees, is 19.6 percent, and early yields have exceeded that rate.

We know that targeted investments in affordable housing can work. And they are certainly needed. According to the Center on Budget and Policy Priorities, America went from a nationwide surplus of 400,000 affordable rental units in 1970 to a shortage of 4.1 million units in 1989. Since then, the situation has gotten worse. In 1991, 79 percent of poor renters pa id more than 30 percent of their income for housing—and 55 percent spent more than half of their household incomes on rent payments.

At the same time, a U.S. Census Bureau study found that more than 80 percent of all renters could not afford to buy even a modestly priced home. Far too many have become "lifers," people who may never realize the dream of homeownership—unless forceful steps are taken to lower the cost barriers that bar them from becoming homebuyers.

The Clinton Administration and HUD are working closely with Congress to make housing more affordable. Last year you permanently extended the low-income housing tax credit and state and local mortgage revenue bonds. The Federal Housing Administration, which next week will celebrate its 60th anniversary, in 1993 had the second best year in its history, insuring more than 1 million mortgages, including 400,000 for first-time homebuyers. At HUD we are working hard to expand the pool of capital for affordable housing through Fannie Mae and Freddie Mac, the Federal Home Loan Bank System, state housing finance agencies, and other sources of investment partnerships. When we began looking around for additional capital sources, it became clear to us that a variety of institutional investors, including pension funds, foundations, university and religious endowments, could certainly expand their portfolios in new directions that are to their financial benefit as well as improving communities.

Pension funds have tremendous resources. Since 1978, pension fund assets have grown 500 percent, to approximately $4.6 trillion today, one-fifth of all financial assets in America.

Only a small proportion of these trillions of dollars are currently invested in housing. According to the Commerce Department, in 1991, just 3 percent of the $783 billion then in public employee pension funds was invested in residential mortgages.

THE SECTION 8 COMMUNITY INVESTMENT DEMONSTRATION

I am proud to discuss with you today HUD's new program designed to build bridges to pension fund managers and forge new investment partnerships for affordable housing. Last year Congress authorized the Section 8 Community Investment Demonstration, an exciting initiative that we are now in the process of implementing. The AFL-CIO Housing Investment Trust helped conceive and refine the idea based on their experience investing in affordable multifamily housing. The basic idea is simple. HUD makes available to pension funds, on a competitive basis, Section 8 project-based rental assistance to support construction and rehabilitation of affordable multifamily housing. This subsidy reduces the risk by ensuring more predictable cash flows from project rents, making pension fund financing more secure both for portfolio yield and more liquid for sale to secondary market investors such as Fannie Mae and Freddie Mac.

Congress has authorized and appropriated $100 million for project-based Section 8 rental assistance certificates, which will leverage many millions of additional dollars from the private sector and state and local investment. While the application process is still open, we have already received applications from the California Public Employees Retirement System working with the

BRIDGE Housing Corporation, the Board of Pensions and Retirement of the City of Philadelphia working with the Philadelphia Redevelopment Authority, the New York City Comptroller's Office (on behalf of the New York City Employees Retirement System, the Police Pension Fund, and the Teachers Retirement System), and Equitable Real Estate Investment Management representing special economically targeted investment funds (Community Works Fund, California Community Mortgage Fund) with pension fund investors ranging from the St. Louis Carpenters Pension Fund to CalPERS to the Los Angeles Fire and Police Pension Fund to the Massachusetts Bay Transit Authority Retirement Fund.

The CalPERS application is a reflection of a sea change that is beginning to take place among pension funds as awareness grows of good business opportunities based on meeting key economic and social needs. CalPERS is one of the investors in the World/BRIDGE initiative, along with World Savings, the California State Teachers Retirement System (CalSTERS), the Bank of America, Wells Fargo Bank, and the Ford Foundation. Together they are committing more than $300 million in financing for the BRIDGE Housing Corporation, the nation's largest non-profit developer of affordable housing. Bridge will use the funds to build 5,000 homes for low- and moderate-income residents in northern and southern California communities oven the next three years. The pension funds are making construction loans to get these rental and homeownership developments built throughout the state.

HUD is currently expecting to receive numerous additional applications for the Section 8 Community Investment Demonstration funds, including from the AFL-CIO Housing Investment Trust. The Trust solicited project proposals to package investments for its own application to HUD, and it received 191 proposals to build or rehabilitate over 21,000 affordable housing units, more than half of them to be for Section 8 tenants. These proposals cover 34 states and 110 cities, from California to Florida, Maryland to Massachusetts Virginia to Wisconsin, New Jersey to Illinois, Texas to Michigan, and more.

The Section 8 Community Investment Demonstration is already generating so much competitive interest from pension funds that it will clearly produce many thousands of affordable housing units, by leveraging the Section 8 certificates with additional private sector and state and local government financing. As a consequence, we have asked for a much larger $400 million authorization and appropriation for Fiscal Year 1995. We believe that as the word gets out to the pension community, the level of competitive demand for this initiative will grow substantially, and HUD should be prepared to accommodate a greater number of the many worthwhile applications that may come from a wide range of new investors.

THE TARGETED PENSION FUND SALE OF FHA MORTGAGE ASSETS

HUD's role in fostering pension fund partnerships, begun last year with the Community Investment Demonstration, is now extending its reach to other means of generating economically targeted investments and leveraging federal resources.

We are currently designing a new plan to encourage targeted pension fund investments in low and moderate income housing, this time through our FHA mortgage sales program.

Beginning next fiscal year, HUD will sell at auction a major portion of its $8 billion portfolio of multifamily mortgages. These mortgages were originally private loans insured by FHA, but are now owned by the Department. As real estate markets began declining in the 1980s, HUD faced the same problems as commercial banks, insurance companies and other financial institutions.

HUD's challenge is to do a good job with FHA's primary mission—providing credit enhancement for the affordable housing market and servicing our mortgage insurance portfolio—while at the same time managing our growing inventory of repossessed loans and foreclosed properties. As I have testified on previous occasions, we are responding to this changing environment by creating a new HUD that is not bogged down in property management, but instead is focused on successfully expanding and efficiently servicing FHA-insured mortgages.

As part of our efforts to reinvent HUD, we intend to utilize the new distressed loan and property markets created by the Resolution Trust Corporation, the FDIC, and various private institutions. These organizations have identified a pool of buyers interested in working out and servicing nonperforming loans. We plan to auction our nonperforming portfolio of FHA mortgages to buyers better qualified than HUD to deal with these troubled loans. Our goal of moving this entire portfolio into private hands will be balanced with two other goals: (1) preserving the nation's assisted housing stock and (2) respecting the needs of tenants in that housing and the communities in which they live.

Approximately $750 million of the FHA mortgage portfolio is secured by properties receiving partial government subsidies, but not enough to qualify as "subsidized properties." Many of these properties are mixed income apartment projects still in good shape, that could benefit from mortgage servicing by experienced private sector institutions. HUD would prefer that such institutions are long-term investors sensitive to the preservation of these properties as decent, affordable housing and to enhancing the community environment. We believe that a good way to accomplish this objective is through joint venture sales to pension funds. Targeted sales of these mortgages can provide a sound market investment for pension funds able to provide the appropriate servicing and management.

This summer, HUD officials will meet with leaders in the pension fund community to discuss potential market interest in purchasing our loan portfolio. We seek to do business with pension funds wanting to expand their capacity and expertise to engage in profitable, long-term investments in affordable housing. Based on our initial research, we are optimistic about the prospects for success. Completing a targeted mortgage sale to pension funds in 1995 will do more than streamline FHA and make HUD more efficient. It will ensure stable servicing for a $750 million portfolio of low and moderate income multifamily housing, and leverage federal resources by helping to establish new sources of capital for community investment.

HUD'S 108 PROGRAM AND SECURITIZING CDBG LOANS: TARGETED COMMUNITY INVESTMENTS IN ECONOMIC DEVELOPMENT AND AFFORDABLE HOUSING

With the help of Congress, HUD has recently revived and Strengthened the Section 108 loan guarantee program. This program enables state and local governments that are entitled by formula to receive Community Development Block Grants, to borrow in the capital markets with HUD providing loan guarantees backed by the collateral of future CDBG allocations. The funds may be used for economic and business development, infrastructure improvement, affordable housing, and other job creation and community revitalization purposes.

HUD recently established the Economic Development Initiative (EDI) to encourage local communities to leverage private capital using the 108 loan guarantees. EDI provides competitive grants for 108 users to help write down interest costs and establish loan loss reserves for debt repayment. Pension funds and-other institutional investors are now beginning to provide financing for Section 108 projects. In Worcester, Massachusetts, the AFL-CIO Building Investment Trust acted as the lender on a Bio-Tech research facility using 108 loan guarantees, and is also making the 108-guaranteed loan to construct one of only two new office buildings in south central Los Angeles in the last three decades. In Boston, Fidelity Investments, the largest mutual fund in the U.S. with more than $200 billion in assets, has invested $26 million in equity capital in the new World Trade Center Hotel and Garage, which is being financed using a Section 108 loan guarantee. The project is expected to create 325 permanent jobs, in addition to the construction-related employment.

The Department has also hired consultants offering technical assistance for local governments to explore better ways of gaining access to new sources of capital, including selling pools of CDBG small business and economic development loans as securities to secondary market investors. In April the State of South Carolina's Jobs and Economic Development Authority Securitized the future income stream of loan repayments from a CDBG-funded small business revolving loan program, and sold the first lien security to the MacArthur Foundation for $7.4 million. The MacArthur Foundation obtained a safe and competitive return for an economically targeted investment in local economic development, and South Carolina received an immediate infusion of funds to reinvest in community revitalization. The proceeds of this sale will be used for small business loans that will create 300 new jobs and leverage an additional $11 million in private investment. This economic development loan securitization is a new model for HUD. Additional CDBG small business revolving loan security sales are being arranged in Miami and Denver, with Citibank as a potential purchaser in Miami.

One point to emphasize with the MacArthur Foundation deal in South Carolina is that there are other types of institutional investors, not just pension funds, that can be draw into affordable housing and community development. The Council on Foundations estimates that philanthropic foundations have a total investment portfolio of $163 billion. This does not compare with the $4.6 trillion of pension fund assets, but if even a small portion of foundation endowment funds were invested in community improvement, it would make a tremendous difference. Many foundations do engage in Program-related investments, but the MacArthur Foundation's purchase of the economic development loan securities may help open up a potentially broader market for community-oriented capital. University and hospital endowment funds, not yet reached by HUD's efforts, are another potentially rich source of capital for economically targeted investing.

On Monday, HUD and Fannie Mae co-sponsored a day-long meeting to explore new capital sources and instruments to invest in local communities. Included in the meeting were representatives of foundations and university endowments. Today we are hosting a conference at HUD on religious leadership in urban communities. We have begun identifying the endowments of major religious institutions that could potentially create new partnerships for community investment.

CONCLUSION

The potential for affordable housing and community development—and for secure investment opportunities—is simply tremendous.

It's also a powerful example of what we can accomplish when the public and private sectors work creatively together. In President Clinton's government, we see this kind of public- private partnership as the wave of the future.

HUD's new pension fund initiative is just one aspect of a much broader Clinton Administration strategy for community revitalization. It's a strategy that builds across the board on partnerships—between federal, state and local governments, private industry and nonprofit organizations.

It's also a strategy that builds from the bottom up; that seeks to harness the creative ideas, the entrepreneurial skills, and the commitment of people in communities—elected officials, public servants and civic leaders, business people, community. activists, and individual residents.

It's a strategy that focuses on concrete results: block by block, neighborhood by neighborhood, community by community—changing the face of public housing; leveraging investment in more affordable rental housing; opening doors to homeownership; promoting commercial development; creating jobs.

You'll find this strategy expressed in virtually every initiative we're undertaking: reducing homelessness; remaking public housing; expanding homeownership and affordable housing; investing in community development, and encouraging Empowerment Zones and Enterprise Communities.

It is first, foremost and throughout a strategy for investment in our nation. It's a strategy that can only succeed with the full participation of America's business and financial institutions.

Affordable housing can yield a sound rate of return. It can be a secure investment, a good investment for pension funds.

But beyond that, it's a smart investment for America, because it's an investment in our people. It's an investment that complements the positive entry on the financial balance sheet with a profound human payoff: better housing, more cohesive families, and stronger communities where children can grow up with hope for the future.

Chairwoman Boxer, we appreciate your taking the initiative to call this important hearing. California is so often on the cutting edge of new ideas, and at HUD we share your spirit of innovation, adventure, and challenge. The task before us in the 1990s is enormous: to create the economic conditions that enable each individual in every community to have the opportunity to live in good health, peace and prosperity. It will cost a lot to achieve this goal. To succeed will depend a great deal on fully mobilizing individual and community responsibility, but it will also require considerable financial capital even to make a dent in some of the most intractable problems. We are now embarking on a course that will find and encourage new partners to step up to the plate. We are pleased to have Senator Boxer, Chairman Mfume and the members of the Joint Economic Committee as our allies as we move forward in this uncharted journey. Thank you, and I am happy to answer any questions.

PREPARED STATEMENT OF MR. COYLE

I. Introduction

Members of the Committee, my name is Stephen Coyle, and I am the Chief Executive Officer of the AFL-CIO Housing Investment Trust, and Chairman of the Policy Development Committee of the AFL-CIO Building Investment Trust. I want to thank you for the opportunity to appear before you today to testify regarding the question of how to facilitate pension fund investment in economic development.

I commend the committee for calling hearings on this timely topic. At $4.8 trillion, pension funds are undeniably a major force in the U.S. economy. These institutions comprise almost one third of the financial assets in the country, and their investment decisions significantly impact the allocation of the nation's investment capital. In fact, pension funds make $1 trillion in new investment decisions each year.

No process to develop strategies that will stimulate our sluggish economy, rebuild the nation's cities, promote emerging industries, and strengthen our international competitiveness is complete unless the role of pension funds in the economy is examined.

II. Pension Funds and Targeted Investments

As a general rule, pension fund investment decisions, like most investment decisions, are made without an explicit understanding of their impact on the economy. During the 1980s, however, many pension funds began to question the relationship between their investment activities and the communities around them. Were pension funds fueling the corporate takeovers that left companies over leveraged and unemployment in their wake? Were pension funds investing overseas in companies that compete with U.S. industries and thus export U.S. jobs? Were pension funds overlooking viable investments in America's communities, such as affordable housing and small business ventures? Were funds too passive and, too narrow in their view of what would have a positive impact on plan participants?

In response, some pension funds began to reevaluate the entire range of investment policies and opportunities. Many began to seek out investments that would have a positive economic benefit visible in their communities. At the same time, their goal was to protect the integrity of the funds by earning appropriate rates of return commensurate with risk. The term "economically-targeted investment" was coined to represent this type of investment approach: namely, prudent competitive investments that bring collateral economic benefits.

Jointly-trusted multiemployer pension funds, today comprising approximately $400 billion, have concentrated their targeted development investing efforts on financing residential and commercial real estate projects that create union jobs for plan participants. More than $4 billion of these types of investment's have been made to date.

Public employee pension funds, comprising more than $1 trillion, have looked at a broader array of development initiatives that include small business loans, venture capital, and private placements. However, their primary focus on development investing has been in real estate, and particularly in the single-family residential housing market. According to one 1993 study, public employee funds had $19.8 billion in ETIs, with 64 percent of that amount in housing investments.

Also, to facilitate certain targeted development investments, some pooled investment intermediaries have emerged for pension funds. Through these vehicles, pension funds can rely on the expertise of the intermediary to make investments for them. The AFL-CIO Housing and Building Investment Trusts fall into this category.

The experiences of pension funds with these investments shows that they can work, and that they represent a realistic way to satisfy the duties of the fiduciary while meeting the responsibilities of the citizen. As you have heard from Department of Labor speakers, regulators believe that properly structured targeted development investments can be appropriate for private-sector pension funds, and can have a positive impact on the overall economy.

It is noteworthy that, in spite of the successes of these targeted investments in achieving performance goals and stimulating local economies, private sector single employer pension funds, which make up almost three quarters of all U.S. pension assets, are not active in this market. This fact is worthy of greater attention by this Committee.

Perhaps the primary reason ETIs are such a relatively small part of pension investment activity is due to an overriding perception in the pension community that to consider any impact of an investment beyond risk and return considerations is a direct violation of their fiduciary duty. Furthermore, there is the companion belief that such targeted investments result in reduced returns to the funds.

These are not the views held by the Department of Labor, and Secretary Reich must be commended for making us all rethink our assumption about these important questions.

However, for policymakers seeking to establish incentives that will encourage pension funds to pursue such economic development investments, minimum conditions must be met. Clearly, ERISA fiduciaries and their local counterparts—the people who make the investment decisions—prefer lower-risk, liquid and secured investments. Policies that ignore these constraints will fail.

In fact, these ideas are reflected in the conclusions of a recent study by the U.S. General Accounting Office. In *Pension Plans—Investments In Affordable Housing Possible with Government Assistance*. GAO concluded that to encourage pension funds to invest in multifamily affordable housing, policymakers should consider pension funds' ability to invest in liquid securities, the presence of government assistance in the form of subsidized funds and investment safeguards. The study also pointed to the important role a financial intermediary can play in making particular investments.

III. AFL-CIO Investment Trusts

These three elements—liquidity, appropriate guarantees and subsidies, and investment intermediaries—guide recent initiatives of the AFL-CIO Housing and Building Investment Trusts.

The AFL-CIO Housing Investment Trust (HIT) is a pooled, commingled fund that was created 30 years ago to provide pension funds a vehicle for making secure investments in housing built with union labor. The AFL-CIO Building Investment Trust (BIT) was established in 1988 to invest pension funds in industrial and commercial ventures. Today, combined Trust assets have risen to more than $1.2 billion. In the past 30 months, more than $1 billion of direct investment has been made by the two Trusts.

HIT's five-year net annualized rate of return was 11.2 percent as of year-end 1993, and BIT has yielded a 7.09 percent net annualized rate of return since inception. More than 400 union staff, multiemployer and public employee pension funds are current investors in the Trusts.

Recently, both HIT and BIT have attempted to utilize federal incentives offered through the U.S. Department of Housing and Urban Development to accommodate pension fund investors' concerns. Let me now outline strategies that produce investments that offer benefits to communities, that at the same time achieve appropriate returns for investors.

IV. Community Investment Demonstration Program and the National Partnership for Community Investment: An Example of Securitization

To encourage pension fund investment in multifamily affordable housing, last year Congress enacted the Community Investment Demonstration Program. HIT will participate in the first round of this Program. The Program earmarks $100 million in Section 8 project-based housing subsidies exclusively for pension investors that finance the construction or rehabilitation of affordable multifamily rental or limited equity co-op housing. Notably, the demonstration is the first federal program which offers incentives exclusively to pension fund investors. HUD Secretary Henry Cisneros and the Congress deserve credit for taking this important first step.

In creating the Program, Congress was responding to a shortage of capital to finance affordable multifamily housing. The dwindling supply of affordable housing has reached critical levels. Further, a severe credit crunch has hindered developers from building new units, with new apartment construction at its lowest level in decades. This shortage of decent rental units resulted in skyrocketing housing costs for many Americans.

The Demonstration Program is designed to provide direct rental assistance for low-income renters to make housing affordable. At the same time, however, the Section 8 subsidies serve as powerful incentives for the private sector, and pension funds specifically, to finance new housing production.

This arrangement promotes the securitization of multifamily housing loans'. Briefly, a potential pension fund lender can include expected Section 8 rental income directly for terms of five to fifteen years in cash flow analyses for new construction or rehabilitation. The predictability of the Section 8 cash flow attracts the securitization of the loans by Fannie Mae or Freddie Mac. This securitization reduces the investment risk, increases liquidity, and encourages pension funds to invest in affordable multifamily housing production.

In response to the legislation, the AFL-CIO Housing Investment Trust solicited proposals from housing development groups across the country. The response was overwhelming. Some 195 proposals have been returned, requesting financing for 21,383 housing units with a total of $1.5 billion in total development activity. Clearly, the need for this program is real. There is capacity across the country to build these projects. The time to act is now.

Not only is there tremendous demand for the Section 8 subsidies, but proposals received thus far reflect many creative uses of available funding that will maximize housing affordability and new production. As such, Trust financing and the rental assistance on the projects would significantly leverage other public and private financing sources.

Below are examples of proposals that will make up the pipeline that Housing Investment Trust will submit to HUD:

- Along the length of the Rio Grande River Valley in Texas, where hundreds of thousands of people live in poverty-stricken "colonias", the Trust is working with HUD, local community organizations and officials to create a model of how existing resources can be otter utilized to provide decent, safe housing.

- The renovation of an existing hotel in the Central City East area of Los Angeles has been proposed to create 65 single-room occupancy units for homeless individuals. The sponsor is an experienced non-profit organization that is nationally-known for its work developing and managing housing for the homeless. The Trust has beef asked to provide a $1.4 million loan, that will leverage an additional $2.5 million in funds from the Low Income Housing Tax Credit Program and the city of Los Angeles.
- Contributing to a broad-based revitalization effort in the Sandtown/ Winchester neighborhood of Baltimore, approximately 136 units of family housing could be rehabilitated through $3.5 million in HIT financing. Section 8 assistance is being sought for half of those units. This exciting project would help stabilize the surrounding community, and reinforce the substantial public and private investments which have been made recently in the area.
- The Trust is reviewing an innovative proposal from the state of New Jersey to provide scattered-site housing for people with HIV/AIDS and their families. Long-term commitments from the State for necessary support services would be an integral component of the initiative.

A number of pension funds and other intermediaries have applied for funding under' this Program. By all accounts, within ninety days, of publishing the Notice of Funds Availability, the $100 million will be committed. Congress should appropriate and authorize more funds for this vital program.

V. HUD section 108 Program: Pension Funds and Economic Development

Developing ways to securitize commercial and economic development investment by pension funds is more challenging. The AFL-CIO Building Investment Trust has begun initial efforts in this area in the past 18 months. Let me review two examples.

One commercial project financed by BIT, and a second project that will soon be financed, utilize an existing federal program to support commercial ventures that have significant stimulative impact on the community.

They rely on the loan guarantee provision of the Community Development Block Grant program, through the Section 108 program. Common to both projects is the fact that without the federal guarantees, they would not have been financed and built.

Worcester Biotechnology Research Building
Worcester, MA

This project, a 93,000 square foot research building, was constructed in Worcester, Massachusetts, and now houses several biotech firms engaged in various medical technologies. Initially, while the prospective tenants in the proposed research building had promising new technology, their credit was relatively weak. This is not unusual for venture biotech firms. Because the industry has tremendous potential for growth and future job creation, the community of Worcester was enthusiastic to assist the project. However, conventional private financing sources had already rejected financing requests.

Representatives of the BIT met with community officials to discuss how the development could proceed. By using the Section 108 funds to provide an initial guarantee of BIT financing, the project got off the ground. Because this was the first time that the Section 108 program was structured as this type of guarantee, many legal issues arose that required resolution with HUD, the community of Worcester, and BIT.

An innovative financial package was negotiated to allow the project to proceed and provide flexibility to the City of Worcester. One significant aspect of the financing package is the partial release of the guarantee when certain negotiated performance parameters are met. In effect, as the project proves itself economically viable over time, the government guarantee will be removed. This accomplished two important objectives:

1. It allowed private capital to take on more of the risk of the project as the project proved to be economically successful or met performance standards; and
2. The Section l08 funds allocated to this project would not necessarily be tied up for the life of the project, and could be used again, on a future development project once released.

The Economic Development Department Building Los Angeles, CA

This 26,900 square foot office building will be constructed at 54th and Crenshaw in South Central Los Angeles, representing the second new office building financed in the area since the disturbances of 1992. (The first was also financed utilizing BIT pension fund financing and public sector guarantees).

Before allocating Section 108 funds to this project, all parties wanted to be sure that development was economically feasible. Here, BIT worked with the developer, the community, the State of California and the City of Los Angeles to structure and underwrite a financially viable venture. Relying on its private market expertise, BIT assisted in the lease negotiations, secured a long-term tenant, helped to define the construction budget and assisted in selecting qualified contractors.

Through this process, a comfort level was achieved that resulted in the city's commitment of the Section 108 funds to the project to guarantee the pension investment in economic development.

VII. Role of the Government Incentives: Section 8 Subsidies and Section 108 Loan Guarantees

These two existing federal programs have been utilized by HIT and BIT to structure financing in ways that make the investment yield competitive returns while addressing the fiduciary concerns of pension funds. Through them, pension capital is encouraged to invest in economic and housing development that results in affordable housing, promotes good paying jobs, and supports businesses that must be the employment generators of our economy and the key to international competitiveness. At the same time, there was no sacrifice of investment return for investors.

The Section 8 subsidy program demonstrates the use of a federal subsidy to create a replicable system of finance through increased securitization of multifamily investments. The Worcester Biotechnology project and the Economic Development Building in Los Angeles utilize the Section 108 loan program to support small- and medium-sized businesses that are in need of investment capital that can create the jobs we need and the technology to compete globally.

There are many more deserving projects that can provide affordable housing and economic development that could benefit from expansion and perhaps retooling of these two HUD programs. Congress should expand and strengthen these programs, so that more pension fund capital will consider affordable housing and economic development investments.

However, in a broad sense, government incentives alone will not create the housing, jobs, technology, and innovation that is essential to stimulating the, economy. To be most effective, incentives must be tied to the engine of the private sector, as these two HUD programs have attempted. As Harvard Business School's Michael Porter points out, for instance, direct subsidies are only beneficial if they are used as signals of directions for appropriate behavior. The private sector must step in to complete these tasks.

In conclusion, the vital role that pension funds play in the U.S. economy can no longer be ignored. As described above, there are many multiemployer and public employee pension funds that recognize this fact, and have been successfully pursuing investments that can bring an ancillary benefit to local communities, while fully meeting their fiduciary responsibilities.

Clearly, there is a role for government in encouraging the private sector to finance investments that strengthen our communities. The Department of Labor should be applauded for its recent efforts to dispel myths surrounding these "ETIs", and promote the acceptance of this type of investing. Some federal programs, such as the HUD Section 8 and Section 108 program can support this type of investing as well.

However, more can be done. These hearings will begin the process of defining what new directions the emerging public/private partnerships for pension investments will take.

Members of the Committee, the AFL-CIO Housing and Building Investment Trusts look forward to working with you in examining these proposals.

I would be happy to respond to any questions. Thank you.

PREPARED STATEMENT OF MR. CRIST

The California Public Employees' Retirement System (CalPERS) is the largest public employee retirement system in the United States and the third largest pension fund in the world. CalPERS currently has approximately $80 billion in its trust fund, which is administered by a thirteen member Board of Administration serving as fiduciaries for more that 970,000 members.[1]

Article XVI of the California Constitution assigns the CalPERS Board of Administration plenary authority and the sole and exclusive fiduciary responsibility for investment of monies and administration of the system "... in a manner that will assure prompt delivery of benefits and related services to the participants and their beneficiaries." Our State's Constitution also requires that the assets of CalPERS "... are trust funds and shall be held for the exclusive purposes of providing benefits to participants in the retirement system and their beneficiaries ..." California's Constitution further requires that the members of the CalPERS Board of Administration "... shall discharge their duties with respect to the system solely in the interest of, and for the exclusive purposes of providing benefits to, participants and their beneficiaries, minimizing employer contributions thereto, and defraying reasonable expenses of administering the system" and that the "... Board's duty to its participants and their beneficiaries shall take precedence over any other duty."

Representing CalPERS as President of the Board of Administration, I wish to begin this testimony by assuring the Joint Economic Committee that our Board fully understands the requirements of the California Constitution, and that each member of the Board exercises the utmost care, skill, prudence and diligence in carrying out their fiduciary responsibilities. With this in mind, I will share with you the nature and focus of our policy on economically targeted investments, the extent of our commitment to such investments and the reasons we are able to make such commitments.[2]

CalPERS operates under an investment policy designed to generate the best possible total return on a long-term basis at an acceptable level of risk. Because the comparative performance of the different sectors invested in by CalPERS varies extensively over any given length of time, the CalPERS portfolio is well diversified.[3] Returns in the form of income and capital gains are determined by the level of activity and profitability of the economic sectors in which investments are made, both domestically and internationally.[4]

---

[1] CalPERS has more than 970,00() members, of which approximately 280,000 are retired and receiving benefits. The remaining 690,000 active members are either working as employees covered by the system, or have changed employment but left their pension assets in the fund, planning to ultimately receive benefits. CalPERS active members include state government employees, nonteaching school employees and other public agency employees. The public agency members are employed by approximately 1 ,300 separate contracting agencies, such as city and county governments and other special governmental entities.

[2] The CalPERS Board of Administration has high funding standards. At the present time, the $80 billion trust fund is sufficient to pay about 93% of all current and future promised benefits. Last year, CalPERS paid out mere than $3 billion in retirement and death benefits, a little over $250 million per month. These benefits were funded by investment income (67%), employer contributions (18%), and employee contributions (15%).

[3] CalPERS' current statement of fund assets is presented in Appendix 1.

[4] CalPERS provides a defined benefits retirement system. CalPERS, like most other U.S. pension systems, employs the level funding method for funding its liabilities, which properly provides for future liabilities by actuarially determining the contribution rates necessary to pay future benefits.

Economically targeted investments (ETIs) are most commonly defined at the present time as investments "designed to produce a competitive rate of return commensurate with risk as well as to create collateral economic benefits for a targeted geographic area, group of people or sector of the economy."[5] Some investors will argue that ETIs are no more than "social investments" which would not be made by prudent fiduciaries because they are based partially on considerations other than those in the immediate best interests of the owners of the assets. It is clear to us at CalPERS, however, that the present and future financial health of our trust fund is inextricably related to the economic health of California. Beyond the obvious microeconomic analysis that is required to make specific investment decisions it is not only necessary for us, as prudent fiduciaries, to simultaneously consider macroeconomic conditions, it is necessary for us to consider the macroeconomic implications of our investments. In other words, it is not just acceptable to consider what are referred to as the collateral economic benefits of any investment, it would be imprudent not to include such considerations in the investment decision making process.

CalPERS adopted an ETI policy in April, 1993.[6] The geographic area focused on in the policy's definition of ETIs is, of course, California. The policy statement identifies ten guidelines for ETI investment, including no concession of risk and cost adjusted return, no distortion of our established overall asset allocation and geographic diversification guidelines, and strict quarterly performance evaluation requirements based on market prices. Our system's ETI investments are distinguished by the fact that they represent investments that are undertaken within California and are not merely part of a broader investment strategy in national or international markets. We do not consider or account for our ETIs as a separate asset class with a specific asset allocation or a separate target rate of return. Rather, investments that one might identify as ETIs may be in made in any asset class as long as they can be made with risk-adjusted market rate of return expectations. There is no downgrading of investment quality contemplated, implied, or assumed in any ETI opportunity approved by CalPERS. To do so would violate CalPERS' ETI policy and fiduciary standards.

The primary impact of CalPERS' ETI policy has been, and probably will continue to be, in three asset classes: real estate, alternative assets and private equity. Funds committed to ETI projects, funds leveraged into the projects and the resulting total investments by asset category are shown in Table 1.

---

[5] *Economically Targeted Investments. A Reference for Public Pension Funds*, (Institute for Fiduciary Education, Sacramento, California, June, 1993), p. 5.

[6] CalPERS' ETI Policy Statement is presented in Appendix 2.

Table 1 CalPERS ETI INVESTMENTS

Asset Class	Committed	Leveraged	Total
Real Estate			
Affordable Housing	$200,000,000	$ 90,000,000	$ 290,000,000
Single Family Housing	$633,000,000	$735,000,000	$1,368,000,000
Acquisition & Development*	$100,000,000	$0	$ 100,000,000
Commercial	$515,000,000	$0	$ 515,000,000
Alternative	$ 200,000	$77,000,000	$ 277,000,000
Private	$0	$0	$0
Totals	$1,648,000,000	$902,000,000	$2,550,000,000

* $400,000 has been allocated to A&D, but only $100,000,000 committed to date.

Real estate ETI investments in the CalPERS portfolio consist of single family housing construction, affordable housing mortgages, residential acquisition and development financing and commercial mortgages. The single family housing program, established in 1992, has committed $633 million for 64 projects building 7,734 units. CalPERS has committed $50 million to the Equitable California Community Mortgage Fund and $150 million to the Bridge Housing Corporation for the purpose of being part of large public-private partnerships working to provide affordable multifamily housing and neighborhood retail, industrial and commercial facilities in underserved communities. Both the California Community Mortgage Fund and the Bridge/ World Housing Fund are currently applying to HUD for Section 8 Community Investment Demonstration Program participation Through these associations CalPERS thus joins the New York City pension funds and the New York City Community Preservation Corporation as the only applicants in the first round of competition for HUD's Section 8 program. CalPERS believes in the value of public-private funding partnerships and is convinced that both good returns and improved economic conditions will result from these projects.

CalPERS has an Alternative Emerging Investment (AEI) portfolio as part of our alternative investment asset allocation. The AEI portfolio provides venture capital and other private investments to funds investing in new, unique or nontraditional strategies. In October, 1993, the CalPERS investment Committee adopted an Alternative Assets Policy for California-Oriented Investment as a specific focus for the AEI portfolio. Included in the approximately $500 million committed to AEI, those funds employing California-oriented strategies have received $200 million. Our California-Oriented Policy commits CalPERS to be proactive with regard to seeking out investment opportunities that are intended to stimulate the California economy and promote job growth while earning superior investment returns. We have found such opportunities that otherwise would have gone undiscovered in this very inefficient market, and will continue to search for more.

While CalPERS currently has no funds committed to ETIs in our private equity asset allocation, we believe that private equity placements may offer the best long-term opportunity to deploy capital for job-creating projects on a large scale. We have had one such opportunity under extensive review, and intend to seek other projects of the same magnitude within our $2.4 billion allocation to private equity.

CalPERS is also committed to placing investments with funds that are controlled by minorities, women or California disabled veterans. Our fund is also interested in strategies emphasizing investment in businesses owned by minorities and women. To date, CalPERS has invested $190 million in such funds.

In addition to the substantial involvement of CalPERS in ETI activities described above, our system is currently doing extensive research in cooperation with other institutional investors to find innovative ways to expand the number and quality of investment grade securities needed to finance public infrastructure. CalPERS is working closely with the Council of institutional Investors to move ahead in a nationally-based working group on infrastructure financing and credit enhancement. This working group is reviewing the recommendations of the Infrastructure Financing Commission regarding federal incentives and state revolving funds to stimulate institutional investment at market rates of return. in California, CalPERS is exploring opportunities for credit enhancement that can lower borrowing costs to public agencies which are CalPERS member employers (i.e., state government, cities, counties and other special districts) while providing acceptable risk-adjusted returns to our trust fund.

One of the greatest obstacles to positive State and Federal government involvement has been a lack of imagination and a tendency to look at the vast assets of public pension funds as a cost-free source of capital funds. Past experiences with different types of so-called "raids" on pension funds and unwarranted political pressure on some funds to make social investments have made good fiduciaries very skeptical regarding any proposals by employers, public or private. CalPERS has been a leader in fighting to protect and grow the fund we hold in trust for the working people who rely on us totally to protect their promised pension benefits. We will work against any attempt by government to raid our fund using any device within imagination and we will not agree to invest any portion of the fund in what have chosen to call PTIs, politically targeted investments.

Having delivered this important political message, let me make the record clear that CalPERS' experiences with ETIs have been rewarding to this point. Further, it is our opinion that with the positive actions and attitudes of the current Secretary of Labor and the current Secretary of Housing and Urban Development, an increased use of public-private partnerships will provide the on-going economic stimulus so desperately needed throughout the United States. The rhetoric used by many in the debate over the semantic definition of ETI has created a false controversy. Thoughtful people should be convinced that all long term investments are in one way or another economically targeted. As was pointed out in the first part of this testimony, it is at least short sighted, and perhaps imprudent, for trust fund fiduciaries not to consider what are referred to in contemporary literature as "collateral benefits" when making long-term investment decisions. What can never be tolerated by prudent fiduciaries is to consider only the collateral benefits when deciding how to invest the fund.

Demonstration programs which contain imaginative ways of attracting pension fund investment are useful in that the experience gained will reduce the skepticism generated by other threatening approaches to obtaining the needed capital. New financial instruments will be designed to provide for the funding of needed public infrastructure as the best minds in the institutional investor world are turned to the task of their creation. And pension funds, like

CalPERS, will increasingly seek out the opportunities provided by capital gaps and inefficient markets to invest their assets in ways that generate very favorable risk adjusted market returns while hitting economic targets at the bull's eye. It takes the will to find a way. Help us to have that will by bringing our funds' investment professionals into your midst to work out the details. This hearing is a very general, but valuable, beginning. Thank you for the opportunity to a be part of positive change.

APPENDIX 1

PUBLIC EMPLOYEES' RETIREMENT SYSTEM

ASSET ALLOCATION AS ALLOCATED TO MANAGERS* 4/30/94
($000) (Produced Monthly)

TARGET	MACRO RANGE	CATEGORY	BOOK VALUE	MARKET VALUE	%	ASSET CLASS %	MACRO %
2		CASH EQUIVALENTS					
		AVAILABLE - INTERNAL ACCOUNTS**	NA	636,641	0.82		
		UNAVAILABLE - STO	NA	288,398	0.37		
		TOTAL CASH EQUIVALENTS		925,039	1.19		
		NET RECEIVABLES/(PAYABLES)	NA	306,886	0.39		
		TOTAL CASH AND RECEIVABLES***	1,231,925	1,231,925		1.58	
37		INTERNAL DOMESTIC FIXED					
		BONDS	26,724,850	26,983,295	34.59		
		R.E. MORTGAGE	1,657,409	1,803,037	2.31		
		TOTAL INTERNAL DOMESTIC FIXED	28,382,259	28,786,332		36.90	
4		EXTERNAL INTERNATIONAL FIXED	4,096,183	4,058,339		5.20	
	40/46	TOTAL FIXED INCOME					43.68
33		DOMESTIC EQUITIES					
		INTERNAL DOMESTIC	13,812,729	22,255,213	28.53		
		EXTERNAL DOMESTIC	4,459,645	5,042,682	6.46		
		TOTAL DOMESTIC EQUITIES	18,272,374	27,297,895		35.00	
2		PRIVATE EQUITY	571,200	313,014		0.40	
		EXTERNAL INTERNATIONAL EQUITIES					
9		UNHEDGED	7,220,041	8,596,335	11.02		
3		HEDGED	1,792,233	2,272,107	2.91		
		TOTAL EXTERNAL INTERNATIONAL EQUITI	9,012,274	10,868,442		13.93	
2		ALTERNATIVE INVESTMENTS	381,209	390,053		0.50	
	45/55	TOTAL EQUITY					49.83
8	5/10	REAL ESTATE EQUITY	6,008,844	5,056,755		6.48	6.48
100		TOTAL FUND	67,956,268	78,002,755		100.00	100.00

*SSB workstation preliminary figures.
**Includes cash and cash equivalents held against forward rolls of government and mortgage backed securities
*** Cost basis for cash only available on a total fund basis.

ASSET ALLOCATORS (Market Value)	BRINSON	TCW
Cash	43,657	6,682
Domestic Fixed	42,956	81,183
International Fixed	126,020	208,377
Domestic Equities	242,278	0
International Equities	348,845	588,528
Total	803,756	884,770

INTERNAL FUTURES EXPOSURE	630,940

APPENDIX 2

CALIFORNIA PERS

Investment Office
P.O. Box 2749
Sacramento, CA 95812-2749
(916)326-3400

ECONOMICALLY TARGETED INVESTMENT POLICY

(Adopted by the PERS Board of Administration Investment Committee on April 19, 1993)

I. BACKGROUND

A. DEFINITION

For purposes of this policy Economically Targeted Investments (ETIs) will be defined as investments intended to assist in the improvement of the economic well-being of the state of California (the State), its localities and residents. Economic stimulation includes job creation, development and savings, business creation, increases or improvement in the stock of affordable housing and improvement of the infrastructure.

B. PHILOSOPHY

1. Increased Emphasis on ETIs

The lack of available funding for national and local investment in the infrastructure, coupled with the recent deterioration in the economic and financial condition of the state of California, have served to heighten interest in ETIs. The objective of ETIs is to successfully employ the vast pool of resources resident in pension funds to promote growth and development of the national and regional economies, while still providing competitive risk adjusted rates of return for the pension funds. In this way pension plans can effectively complement or in some cases supplant less efficient government programs. If structured to be fully competitive on a risk and return basis, ETIs will provide collateral economic benefits to targeted geographic areas, groups of people, or sectors of the economy while providing pension funds with prudent investments.

Furthermore prudent investment in ETIs to create jobs, housing and improve the general infrastructure can serve the broad interests of the beneficiaries. By strengthening the State's economy and the well-being of employers, ETIs should help promote the continued maintenance of employer contributions to the California Public Employees Retirement System (CALPERS).

California Public Employees' Retirement System
Lincoln Plaza - 400 P Street - Sacramento, CA 95814

2. The Need for an ETI Policy
A consistent and methodical means of evaluating all ETI opportunities is of paramount importance, because unlike more conventional and standardized investment vehicles, ETIs are not uniform in structure, method or objective. Consequently, a policy to evaluate the risk, return and liquidity characteristics must be established to assure that these investments are comparable on a risk/return basis with more traditional opportunities and are consistent with the financial requirements of CALPERS.

Investment in ETIs may represent a unique opportunity for CALPERS as ETIs have remained virtually unexplored by the larger financial community partly because the opportunities are too small in number or size to elicit broad based institutional investment interest. The lack of homogeneity of these instruments, likewise, make ETIs difficult to market on a large scale basis. ETIs may involve less developed or well understood opportunities which make use of government subsidies or smaller regional investment possibilities. The lack of broad based experience and prior track record further recommend that each ETI be separately evaluated based on its unique structure and potential in accordance with CALPERS standard investment criteria and this ETI Policy. This will help ensure that all CALPERS responsibilities and investment requirements are being addressed in the evaluation and investment process.

The existence of this ETI policy should not be construed as a mandate to invest in ETIs, but rather should be viewed as a set of suggested parameters within which to consider such investments.

C. PROGRAM OBJECTIVE

The Board will consider the secondary objective of promoting economic growth and well being in the state of California and its localities when not in conflict with the Board's duties of loyalty, care, skill, prudence, diligence and diversification . The emphasis will be on the promotion of long term sustainable economic, industry and business growth, job creation and affordable housing.

II. PROGRAM POLICIES

1. The Board's constitutional duties, as defined and clarified by the recent amendments to California Constitution Article XVI, Section 17, take precedence over any other considerations. Any other considerations will be entertained only when not in conflict with any of these duties. Investments made for the sole benefit of the System's beneficiaries may also generate collateral benefit.

2. CALPERS will only consider ETIs which when judged solely on the basis of economic value, would be financially comparable to alternatively available investments. Comparability will be judged on a risk adjusted basis with CALPERS willing to accept no less in return and incur no additional risk or cost.

3. The collateral benefits will not be considered part of the return to CALPERS nor shall any improvement to the State's economy be considered part of risk reduction. The decision to make the ETI and consideration of its broader benefits may only occur after the investment is deemed acceptable to the fund exclusively on its economic investment merits.

4. Any benefit an ETI may confer on other interests (the "target") is not the responsibility or within the ability or control of CALPERS, but only of those who manage or are otherwise responsible for the target enterprise. This will be made expressly clear to third parties and CALPERS beneficiaries.

5. For allocation purposes, ETIs will be included with similar investments that are free of economically targeted elements, and the combined assets will be subject to the Board's asset allocation guidelines, ranges and targets. Investments shall not be made so as to alter the overall risk/return profile of CALPERS investments, which derives from CALPERS liability profile and funding level.

6. ETIs shall not materially alter CALPERS desired level of diversification. Included in the concept of diversification are:
   - The mix of asset types.
   - The exposure to different economic, sector and industry classifications
   - The mix of investment quality

   Particular attention should be paid to the California representation in the CALPERS portfolio. CALPERS exposure to the State's economy, inclusive of investment in ETIs, should generally be in line with California's representation in the eligible investment universe.

7. ETIs must at all times conform to all the laws, requirements, policies and procedures governing CALPERS.

8. Since this will represent an actively managed portion of a portfolio or will itself be an actively managed portfolio, a proper amount of due diligence will be required. This due diligence, to be conducted by Staff, designated outside consultants and/or advisors, will at a minimum address:
    - Legal sufficiency
    - Identification of any potential conflicts of interest
    - Investment Sufficiency - The standard for investment sufficiency will be consistent with existing internal policies and practices of due diligence analysis for each specific asset type.

9. After all the above criteria have been met in the review of ETIs, consideration will be given in order of preference to those investments which may benefit:
    a. Current and retired members of the California Public Employees Retirement System
    b. Residents of the State of California
    c. Enterprises that operate for the benefit, support, or employment of residents of the State of California.
    d. Enterprises that address the economic and social needs of United States residents with unique major representation in the State of California.

10. The ETI investments, whether in a stand-alone portfolio or incorporated with like investments which have no economically-targeted orientation, will be valued at market prices and will be subject to performance measurement at least quarterly.

Prepared by: Hilda Appibaum
Hilda Appibaum
Principal Investment Officer

James E. Burton
JAMES E. BURTON
ASSISTANT EXECUTIVE OFFICER

PREPARED STATEMENT OF MR. SMITH

Chairwoman Boxer and members of the committee, thank you for the opportunity to participate in today's hearing on pension fund investment. I request my full statement be inserted in the record.

Let me begin by briefly introducing myself. I am Executive Director of Excelsior Capital Corporation, a not-for-profit corporation established by New York Governor Mario M. Cuomo to encourage pension funds to make prudent investments that will also help the state's economy and citizens. In addition, the Governor has signed legislation to encourage our public employee pension funds to make targeted investments. In fact, in the past decade over one billion dollars of targeted investments have been made by pension funds in New York. Further, he appointed a Task Force on Pension Funds, chaired by Ira Millstein, whose report, Our Money's Worth, lead to the establishment of Excelsior and sparked increased involvement of pension funds in corporate governance.

Excelsior's mission is to work with public, union, and corporate pension funds by researching and developing new investment programs that help these investors earn a competitive risk adjusted rate of return and provide an additional economic or social benefit.

In my remarks I will make the following points. First, most investments have an economic impact and it is legally appropriate and economically important for pension fund trustees to be conscious of this fact and to seek out ways to target these impacts. Second, there are practical impediments to the adoption of targeted investment programs. These barriers are being overcome, but only slowly, and until recently, with little help from the relevant government agencies.

Lastly, to accelerate the spread of ETIs, we need innovative public policies, including efforts to foster more awareness of the importance of targeted investing.

Before I discuss these points, let me explain what we mean by the term economically targeted investment. While ETIs are similar to other investments in that they are intended to produce a competitive financial return, what differentiates them is the investor's concern and desire to capture the economic impact of the investment. The ETI investor is more demanding, not less, for they want not only an appropriate risk adjusted rate of financial return on their investment, they also seek an identifiable—even quantifiable—economic impact or return.

Let me be more specific. Most investments have an economic impact, distinguishable from its financial return. However, what differentiates ETIs from other investments, is that ETIs focus or target this impact.

This focusing or targeting on economic impact can take many forms. For example, an in-state commercial real estate program employs geographic targeting—allocating an economic benefit to a particular geographic area. A second type of targeting is by social group. For example, to help first time homebuyers, investors have used their clout to get Fannie Mae to lower downpayment requirements and allow higher ratios of debt payment to income. A third type of targeting is by business segment of the private sector. For example, a number of investors have programs to help small business by committing to buy newly formed pools of SBA guaranteed small business loans.

Can pension fund investors capture this economic impact without sacrificing the investments financial returns, thereby giving the fund an economic return in addition to the expected financial return?

We believe it is legally appropriate for pension funds to make targeted investments. With the issuance of the new interpretive bulletin, the Administration has indicated they agree that ETIs are legally sound. Secretary Reich and Assistant Secretary Berg are to be commended for having taken this important step.

In addition to being legally sound, being concerned about both financial and economic returns of pension fund investments is essential given the impact these enormous capital pools can have on the economy. As our single largest source of capital, pension funds are vitally important for the nation's economy. Pension fund officials are stewards for a growing portion of the nation's capital and have a responsibility to consider the impact of their investments: with increased economic power comes increased responsibilities. And by meeting this challenge, pension funds can strengthen themselves as institutions by improving their standing with their participants and the body politic. When pension funds make economically targeted investments, they strengthen their institutions by building support from those key constituencies. By making ETIs that benefit the general economy, pension funds strengthen their political position and buttress the justification for their preferential tax treatment.

Of course it is true that the safety of the funds—the security of the financial benefit for retirees—is fundamental. At the same time, pension fund trustees and the investment managers to whom they have delegated responsibility, must be concerned with the economic impact their actions as investors and owners have on beneficiaries. We believe these two concerns—the security of retirement income and the economic impact of investments—are compatible, not competing goals. Properly structured programs can serve the financial interests of beneficiaries and the interest all of us share—beneficiaries included—in a stronger and more sustainable economy. Moreover, viewed from the long term these goals are identical.

Our public policies are slowly changing to adapt to this new reality. It is no longer sufficient to judge pension funds by the standards of traditional trust doctrine. We have already witnessed the positive impact pension funds can have as owners of public companies. The question is what will it take to realize the same and even greater benefits from targeted investments.

At Excelsior we are trying to meet this challenges by developing market feasible ETIs. Our strategy is to bring together investors from the corporate, public and union sectors, identify areas where they can agree as to the financial needs of investors, and the useful targeted impact to achieve. We then structure the investment and raise the capital to fund the program.

ETIs are gradually becoming more accepted, witness the increasing number of pension funds who have made them and the diverse range of intermediaries who offer them. Another indication of the acceptance of ETIs is the emergence of corporate pension fund ETI investors. In cooperation with our investment manager partner, Alliance Capital, we are now implementing the Excelsior Subordinated Debt and Equity Fund, whose investors include the public and union funds traditionally associated with ETIs, as well as a number of corporate pension funds.

There are many forces that have encouraged this innovation. First, many pension fund managers are becoming familiar with ETIs. As they become more familiar with them their skepticism subsides and many of the perceived risks commonly attributed to ETIs diminish. As risks are much more clearly defined, pension fund managers begin to see ETIs as viable investment alternatives.

Second, the level of sophistication of ETI products has markedly increased. Initially ETIs were basically restricted to mortgage backed securities. However, current ETIs include diverse and complex equity and debt investments tailored to benefit specific populations, geographic areas, and sectors of the economy.

Third, the support of the current Administration has spurred a great deal of investor interest and raised their comfort level. The DOL's new interpretive bulletin which we are discussing today is very important, not only because it clarifies many of the legal misconceptions associated with ETIs, it shows the Administration supports pension funds considering ETIs.

Despite these hopeful signs, it would be a mistake to believe that ETIs are now broadly accepted. ETIs have existed for over a decade and their creation and implementation has often been a slow and arduous task. This type of capital market innovation is not a well developed practice nor is it well understood. For example, it is often thought that ETIs are created from scratch or designed to fill a gap in the capital market—to go where other investors will not go. In our experience, ETIs are more likely to be variations on existing products which are re-engineered to maximize and target the investments' positive benefits. ETIs are part of a constant process of market innovation which can be done in a variety of ways and can take a number of forms. Typically, they require a long process of research and development which preceded the initiation of the investment program. For the innovator to bring the program to the market, it must hold the promise of both competitive risk adjusted returns for the investor and profit for the investment manager. For an investment manager to offer a product to pension funds, the manager needs to know he or she can make a profit on the process of investing the money. Especially when first created, the design and implementation of ETIs is labor intensive and a costly process. Often times ETIs require credit enhancements and the coordination of several different parties that have previously not worked together. Coordinating these various groups is difficult work. And because of this necessary labor intensity and the scale, the net fees from these investments often cannot compete with those of other more established investment products. The high costs to develop ETIs coupled with the limited profitability of the transaction for the intermediary has served as a barrier to the creation of more ETI products.

While it is widely believed that this barrier will be substantially reduced as vehicles become standardized, it is unlikely that this will occur in the near future. The main function of ETIs is to target the benefits of an investment to a specific population, geographic region or sector of the economy. While it is possible to use the same ETI structure that benefited one target to benefit another group, at the very least the investment would require substantial modification. While it Is not necessary to start from scratch with each investment, it is also incorrect to assume that all ETIs are easily transportable.

A second impediment to full acceptance of the legitimacy of ETIs is the lingering presence of mixed signals from the DOL under previous administrations. Many pension fund managers remain skeptical about the legality of ETIs under ERISA. For fund managers the possible negative consequences of an ERISA violation far outweighed the potential benefits of making an ETI. Therefore, past questions about the legality of ETIs under ERISA have been substantial enough to deter fund manager action. I strongly believe that this interpretive bulletin will be effective in correcting many of these misconceptions.

A third impediment to future ETI development is the fact that most fund managers take it as an article of faith that the effects of investments are not their concern. So long as fund trustees continue to show little interest or sense of responsibility for the economic impact of their investments, we are unlikely to see significant increase in targeted investments.

Let me suggest several steps the federal government can take to address the impediments to more ETIs. In order for pension funds to accept ETIs as legitimate investment opportunities they must first understand them. The proposed ETI clearinghouse is a good step. More can be done. An aggressive education and technical assistance program supported by the government would be invaluable. Such a program should include support for basic research and development on new ETIs. By commissioning a series of technical studies on possible ETIs, we could increase the number of available ETI investment opportunities, which in turn would help fund managers become more active ETI investors.

Finally, we do not support legally mandating pension funds to make ETIs. That will only hamper this process by effectively locking pension funds into making ETIs regardless of the available investments. Such a mandate will inevitably result in a general perception that ETIs will not benefit a fund's portfolio.

In conclusion, economically targeted investing has emerged as a vital way for pension funds to fulfill their responsibilities to their diverse stakeholders. By giving pension funds the flexibility to target an investment's beneficial effects, ETIs have allowed pension funds to produce both an economic and a financial returns for plan participants. This fundamental alteration in the way we understand pension fund investing is gradually being incorporated into the legal and philosophical framework in which fund managers operate. Yet, it would be dangerous to overstate our accomplishments. The ultimate goal is for all pension funds to routinely consider both the financial and economic returns of all investments. As such there still exist many impediments to achieving that goal. Whether they achieve their potential will largely depend upon what happens in the private sector. Yet today's issuance of the clarification of ERISA is a major step forward. Your continued interest in this subject is essential if we are to make further progress. Thank you.

PREPARED STATEMENT OF MR. NISKANEN

Senator Boxer and members of the Joint Economic Committee:

My brief remarks today make one simple point: Do not allow private pensions to make "economically targeted investments." These investments, also termed social investments, are best described as politically targeted investments—investments that would not otherwise be made except in response to political direction or pressure.

The case against politically targeted investments is also simple:

1. The performance of public-employee pension funds with such investments has been dismal.
   a) A 1983 study by Alicia Munnell, now the Assistant Secretary of the Treasury for Economic Policy, found that public employee plans with such investments earned from 2 to 5 percentage points less than funds without these investments.
   b) A 1993 study by Olivia Mitchell concludes that "Social investment rules hurt pension fund yields; specifically, public pension plans which mandated that a certain proportion of investments be directed to in-state projects generated much lower returns."
   c) A 1993 study by Roberta Romano found that the greater the political influence on public-employee pension fund investment decisions, the lower the return.
2. As a rule, the teachers, police, and other state and local employees bear the costs of these low yield politically targeted investments. A higher share of total compensation must be set aside to fund the promised pension benefits, reducing the direct wages of public employees. Similarly, if the pension assets are not sufficient to fund the promised benefits, these public funds may go bankrupt with the consequent loss of pension benefits. The rationale for financing politically targeted investments at the expense of public employees has never been made quite clear.
3. For the most part, private pensions have not yet been required to make investments in politically favored groups. Private defined benefit plans are regulated because they are also insured, and the regulations authorized by ERISA are designed solely to assure the safety and soundness off these plans, for the protection of the both the plan participants and the federal pension insurance fund. A large and increasing share of private pensions, moreover, are in defined contribution plans for which each plan participant has the opportunity to choose his or her own fund manager and investment portfolio.

   Until recently, ERISA has been interpreted to preclude investments that are not expected to yield the prevailing rate on other investments of the same risk and liquidity. In November 1992, however, a Department of Labor report discussed a procedure for valuing the "net externalities" of investments as a way of broadening the prevailing rate test to include politically targeted investments. And in September 1993, Olena Berg, the Assistant Secretary of Labor for Pensions and welfare Benefits, announced a more expansive interpretation of the prevailing rate test that would "allow collateral benefits to be considered in making investment decisions where such investments are prudent and provide a competitive risk-adjusted return to the plan." She especially encouraged pension fund investment in firms that invest in their own work force.

So far, this threat to private defined benefit plans is only a cloud on the horizon, but it is a dark and ominous cloud. As with the public employee plans, the direct losses from politically directed investments would be to the plan participants, either in the form of lower wages or a failure of the plan to pay the promised benefits. In this case, moreover, the losses would be shared by the federal pension insurance fund, and ultimately the taxpayer, if the plan fails to pay the guaranteed benefits. Several commentators have suggested that ERISA be broadened to protect public employee pension plans against pressure to invest in politically favored groups. The first priority, I suggest, is to assure that ERISA is administered as intended—to protect the safety and soundness of private defined benefit plans.

4. And finally, for those of us who still care, politically targeted pension investments should be regarded as an unconstitutional taking of private property. And the politicians and officials who endorse such measures should be charged with aiding and abetting an unconstitutional act. Twenty years ago, Congress passed ERISA to protect private pensions against the consequences of irresponsible private pension sponsors. It would be a sad irony if the officials responsible for administering ERISA undermine pensions in the interests of politically targeted investments.

Speaking for most of the American labor force, keep your sticky fingers off my pension. I earned it. I saved it so that I would not be dependent on others after my retirement. I own it. Don't tell me that I should have lower wages or lower retirement income so that someone can play political footsie with my pension plan. If you are so smart to know which investments earn a higher return, put your own money in those investments. Or convince your colleagues to do it up front through the budget by reallocating spending or reducing the deficit. in the meantime keep your sticky fingers off my pension!

84-047 O - 94 (88)